WITHDRAWN

Required Reading Range
Module Reader

academia

An AVA Book

Published by AVA Publishing SA
Rue des Fontenailles 16
Case Postale
1000 Lausanne 6
Switzerland
Tel: +41 786 005 109
Email: enquiries@avabooks.com

Distributed by Thames & Hudson (ex-North America)
181a High Holborn
London WC1V 7QX
United Kingdom
Tel: +44 20 7845 5000
Fax: +44 20 7845 5055
Email: sales@thameshudson.co.uk
www.thamesandhudson.com

Distributed in the USA & Canada by:
Ingram Publisher Services Inc.
1 Ingram Blvd.
La Vergne TN 37086
USA
Tel: +1 866 400 5351
Fax: +1 800 838 1149
Email: customer.service@ingrampublisherservices.com

English Language Support Office
AVA Publishing (UK) Ltd.
Tel: +44 1903 204 455
Email: enquiries@avabooks.com

ISBN 978-2-940373-81-9

10 9 8 7 6 5 4 3 2 1

Design by Create/Reject

Production by AVA Book Production Pte. Ltd., Singapore
Tel: +65 6334 8173
Fax: +65 6259 9830
Email: production@avabooks.com.sg

Animated Performance

Required Reading Range
Module Reader

Nancy Beiman
Foreword by Lynn Johnston

**Bringing imaginary
animal, human and fantasy
characters to life**

Ethical: aware-
ness/
reflect-
ion/
debate

academia

Contents

Foreword by Lynn Johnston

When I was a kid, I'd draw cartoons for my brother and he would laugh and laugh. Having an appreciative audience makes any performance worth doing even when the timing is wrong. It was difficult to concentrate in class when ideas and images fogged my mind. I doodled on everything, made tiny animated figures on the corners of my textbooks and it was a compliment to be called the class clown. Sound effects, word play, sarcastic retorts, facial expressions and goofy behaviour were all part of learning what was later to become a career. Kids like me were not bad, we were just hard to tolerate.

Like others who were classified as 'outsiders', the silly, artistic and outspoken kids sought comfort in the company of like minds. We were an even greater force when we pooled our talents and those teachers who saw the potential in us provided theatre, creative writing and art classes. How we loved the teachers who gave us opportunities to express ourselves. We worked hard for them, drawing, painting sets, memorising lines, composing music and performing. Within the school system, they were rare. We pushed ourselves as hard as we could for them and for the joy of using the gifts we'd been given and did not yet know how to use well.

Years later, these teachers are the ones we remember. These were the people who appreciated our cartoons and comedy. They told us we had talent. We thrived on their encouragement. Our pay-off was laughter and the joy of accomplishment. School wasn't always where our teachers were found, however – cartoonists and comedians we admired became teachers too. We studied their work, recording nuances of expression and subtleties of line. We copied and collected and traded and tried everything... and we continued to stick together. Cartooning is largely self-taught. You can either do it or you can't and if *you can*, you are captive. I became a comic-strip artist, but my dream was to be an animator and now, through my work, I know some really good ones!

Nancy Beiman and I met through the National Cartoonists' Society more that 20 years ago. It was clear that had we been in the same grade, in the same class, we would have been on the inside of the outsiders. She draws for laughs. Seriously.

In the right hands, funny drawings are even funnier when they move. The technology to animate drawings was developed in our lifetime. From black-and-white, hand-drawn *Steamboat Willie* (1928) to the three-dimensional *Ratatouille* (2007), we have come a long way and although the process can be explained, to me it will always be magic. Combine the wonders of technology with the gift of comic illustration and the result is beyond spectacular. One skill is God-given, the other is learned. Both take time and dedicated effort to perfect. Both require the encouragement and direction of a good teacher. Nancy Beiman is one of these.

Since she was a kid (one of the outsiders!) Nancy has been working towards this book. From years of study to years in the industry, her knowledge and her willingness to share it have made her one of the most effective and entertaining teachers on the subject of animation. Her textbooks are used by students everywhere. Her interest in the next generation of animators has become an investment. Her support and encouragement are there to ease you in. Her enthusiasm is genuine. As someone with the gift, I hope you take advantage of the information that's here, turn it into something new and pass it on.

Author, cartoonist and creator of the *For Better or For Worse* comic strip.
www.fborfw.com

We're not in live action any more

'**...The medium of animation is not meant to simulate live action...** See, animation, first of all, **is not earth-bound**. You can exaggerate in every possible way and you can indulge in fantasy. You can do things that are not possible in live action. And if you don't use the strength that exists in animation, then why bother with it?'

– Art Babbitt, award-winning animator, animation director and creator of 'Goofy'. Interview with Nancy Beiman (1979)

Animation, that fascinating combination of technological wizardry, performance, and artistic skill, is also one of the most successful branches of motion pictures. Feature-length animated films, once rare and risky to produce, have flourished and multiplied in recent years as a result of amazing innovations in computer graphics that simplified cumbersome processes and shortened production time. Short animated films have also had a renaissance after being pronounced 'dead' a generation ago due to a revolution in motion picture distribution. It is no longer necessary to search for a distributor or theatre that might be willing to exhibit short animated films. The Internet makes it possible to screen independently produced animated films to a worldwide audience simultaneously. There are more animated film festivals than ever before. And last but not least, the explosive growth of video games has made animation part of daily life for millions of people.

Not bad for a field that was considered to be hopelessly outdated and irrelevant as recently as the 1970s. The renewed interest in animation has also led to an explosion in training courses, college and high-school animation programmes, online tutorials, and animation books. There were only three books on animation in print when I started my studies. Now there are hundreds. So why is there a need for yet another book on animation?

Much existing literature barely touches on the acting possibilities of animation. They discuss *how* to do animation but not *why*. The technique and mechanics of animation may be exhaustively explained, but not the thought processes that make the difference between an animated *exercise* and an animated *performance*; between laborious action analysis and the creation of an imaginary yet believable *living* animated personality. It is the animator's acting that puts the life into character animation and gives it a powerful emotional connection with its audience – so powerful that characters created with pencils, pixels or puppets become as affecting and believable as human actors. The animated films remain evergreen, entertaining audiences who might not have been born when they were originally released.

The computer has greatly simplified animation production and distribution by making production tools affordable for anyone with access to the programs and bandwidth, but it has also led to an increasing amount of animation designed to imitate live action. The dimensional quality of computer graphic animation and the ease of standardisation in computer models when compared to the more mutable designs of hand-drawn animation can be used to recreate rather than caricature reality. This can lead to over-reliance on live-action footage as a guide for animation rather than allowing the animator to create an animated performance based on his or her observation and imagination. It is not the best use of the medium.

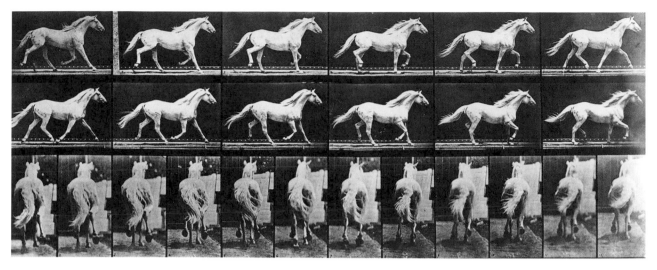

i.ii

Harry Furniss
Illustrator Harry Furniss caricatures the over-the-top acting
of the Victorian period in these images from the *Strand
Magazine*.

Computer graphic animation need be no more 'realistic' than hand-drawn or puppet animation. Its distortions are handled differently, but the potential for stylisation is there – and it is comforting to note that recent CG features have featured more caricatured and stylised characters than formerly.

Studying live action

Animators and cartoonists have been studying live action ever since 1887, when Eadweard Muybridge published photographs of sequential human action in *Animal Locomotion*. In the 1930s, Donald Graham's action analysis classes at the Walt Disney Studio analysed live-action motion pictures produced at other studios. Originally, live-action film was used only as rough reference for observing and caricaturing the actions of actors or animals. The practice of staging and shooting animated scenes with human actors has sometimes led to this reference being used as a crutch – beginning with the original rotoscope and progressing (or degenerating) into motion capture.

One benefit of using live-action film reference is that the performance will be consistent no matter how many times the clip is repeated. But this is also a significant drawback. If every animator uses a Muybridge horse and rider as reference then every animated horse and rider will move like a Muybridge photograph series from 1887.

As it turns out, horsemen ride differently now to how they did in Muybridge's day, as Ellen Woodbury, a skilled animator and equally skilled horsewoman, discusses in Chapter 4 of this book (see page 100). So basing modern animation on Muybridge photographs is rather like modelling your acting performances on the stagey, obvious, over-dramatic acting style of a hundred years ago, rather than on your animated character's thought processes, which will affect its every move and make your performance unique.

An animator runs into different problems when he or she tries to 'act out' the scene themselves. The human body is not nearly as flexible as a cat's or an ape's. Different sexes or species do not move in precisely the same way. Male actors who act out female character actions can inadvertently incorporate masculine movements into the character (and vice versa). Animators who film themselves for each performance may use the same bits of acting 'business' on a variety of animated characters, which can lead to a

sameness in performance. Art Babbitt put it best when I interviewed him at the Richard Williams studio in 1979:

'There used to be a time... when you could look at a scene or two of animation on screen and say, "Oh, that's Joe Zilch's work." Maybe if there was just one character you were involved with, it wouldn't matter; but it would be different... if you had to animate three or four characters in the picture. If they all moved like you that would be too bad, no matter how beautifully you moved.'

And there are some characters that simply do not share a skeletal and muscular similarity with the human form, as Mark Thurman's illustration of the Flour Sack clearly shows.

The acting challenges for an animated character differ from those faced by human actors. The movement of a human body is restricted by natural constraints, while an animated character has no such limitations. Animated characters may express their changing emotional states by stretching, expanding, flying apart or changing into another creature. An emphasis on 'realism' makes the art of animation more and more earth-bound. This book was written to help animation regain its place among the stars. There is no limit to animated performance just as there are no limits to the human imagination. It is not necessary to rely on reality when it is so easy to *surpass* it.

This book is aimed at the advanced student or journeyman animator who is familiar with the basic principles of animation: *squash, stretch*, basic *walk cycles, volume*, basic *dialogue, charting* and *timing*, and *silhouette value*. *Animated Performance* is designed to expand and develop your acting skills, not repeat exercises that can be found in previously published books. It can be read concurrently with any of the recommended titles listed in the Inspiration and Reference section at the end of the book.

Dedication

I am dedicating *Animated Performance* to Frank Thomas, Ollie Johnston and Shamus Culhane. Frank and Ollie wrote *Disney Animation: The Illusion of Life* in 1981. Their book is the animation 'bible' that codified the techniques of Disney-style animation. Shamus Culhane wrote *Animation From Script To Screen*, the best early animation textbook in 1985, and demonstrated how the Disney Studio's methods revolutionised animation in studios around the world. All three men were my friends, and they deserve much credit (along with Walt Disney and many others) for helping to transform animation from a curiosity into a major art form.

I would also like to thank my late mentor and friend Selby Daley Kelly for her years of support and encouragement, and the late Roy E. Disney, who loved the art and artists of animation.

Nancy Beiman
Oakville, Ontario
January 2010

Animation begins where live action gives up.

– Kaj Pindal, award-winning animator, director and writer

i.iii

Anatomic considerations when drawing the flour sack
Not all animated characters benefit from anatomical reference.
© 2008 by Mark Thurman

1

Design for living

In this chapter you will learn how to stage an animated performance in your imagination through the use of rapid sketches, or thumbnails, that allow you to analyse and perform actions that transcend the limitations of the human body or the laws of physics. With this technique you can literally become any creature that you can imagine.

You will also learn how the animated character's emotions and thoughts are communicated through the movement of its entire body. Exercises demonstrate how varying the pose or attitude of the body dramatically changes the animated actor's performance even before facial expressions are added. You will learn to identify characters that are good 'actors' in animation terms. The timing and blocking of action for dialogue scenes is discussed in the third section, along with the use of props as an aid to acting.

Don't try this at home!
You won't always be willing or able to act out your scene before
starting to animate, and chances are you won't find it easy to
perform the movements of three dogs and a man simultaneously.
And peanut butter is messy.

An introduction to thumbnails

Thumbnails (n.) the first ideas or sketches of a designer noted down for future reference.

Sharing the fantasy

Animated characters and stories begin as a spark in the mind of an animator. This spark must then be translated into a medium that can be viewed by other people. Until the happy time when mental telepathy will instantly communicate the animator's thoughts directly into the waiting minds of the audience, the translation from mind to matter to mind(s), no matter what medium is used, begins with the distinctly low-tech method of drawing on paper.

Drawings can be easily changed, they can be shown to large groups of people at the same time, and they do not depend on specific operating systems or become unreadable when technological hardware or software changes. But paper's greatest value is its cheapness. You can make major changes quickly and inexpensively before spending time, money and effort building, animating, painting and rendering your animated characters on paper, on computer, or in puppet form.

Two questions frequently arise when thumbnails are discussed:

1. Since characters are developed in the storyboard phase of an animated film, can storyboards be used for animation thumbnails? (a topic covered in my earlier book, *Prepare to Board!*) *(Answer: No.)*

2. Is there a difference between acting on a storyboard and acting for animation? *(Answer: Yes.)*

Let's analyse some storyboards and compare them with animation thumbnails to see how small changes in a character's body language can create a completely different interpretation of the scene or story.

Storyboards: The animated script

Take a look at Figures 1.1 and 1.2. It is startling to see how the change in one drawing affects the entire story, yet these are only two of the many possible ways to interpret the tiger's reaction to the insult. How differently this sequence might develop if the tiger reacted aggressively, or openly appealed to the other animals, assuming that they were his friends.

None of the storyboards will appear on the screen in the final film. Storyboards are not the animated performance; *they are the script*. Storyboard is mainly concerned with the WHY of a film (telling the story). Animation (along with layout, art direction, and backgrounds) is concerned with HOW the story points are put across. An animator uses storyboards in the same way an actor uses scripts and director's notes. The storyboard sketches show the character's basic attitudes and give the animated film-maker a simple and inexpensive method of exploring character interactions and story development in a film. Storyboards do not exist in the singular. They are always part of a larger project.

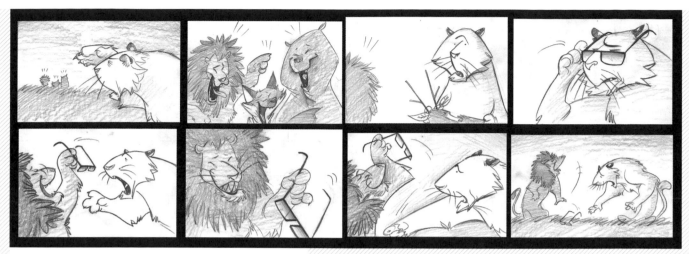

1.1

A storyboard from *How the Tiger Got His Stripes*
This first storyboard excerpt shows a large cat (actually a tiger without stripes) being teased by other jungle creatures who have tricked him into attacking a log. The tiger reacts to the other animals' merriment with blank incomprehension that is in fact due to extreme nearsightedness. He finds his glasses, but is unable to stop the lion from taking and breaking them. Obviously this tiger inspires fear in no one.
© 2008 by Chang Dai

1.2

The tiger's reaction and personality have changed
Here is an alternative version of Panel 4 in Figure 1.1. The tiger's changed body language now gives the scene an entirely different meaning. In the earlier version, the tiger simply peers uncomprehendingly at the other animals through his glasses. Now, he faces away from them, resentful of their unwelcome attentions. A slightly lowered head, raised shoulders, half-shut eyes, a sidelong glance, and a small, downturned mouth have changed this tiger from a hapless nerd into a frustrated, angry predator who is deliberately keeping his emotions in check. But this storyboard drawing was out of character; and so it was replaced.
© 2008 by Chang Dai

Thumbnails: The animated rehearsal

Animation thumbnails translate emotion into motion. The animated performance will develop the character's personality through movement in a scene, or series of animated scenes, after the story has been set. The first step in the animation process involves small, sketchy drawings called 'thumbnails' that codify the most important (key) poses of a character's movements and emotions before the scene is animated. Thumbnails also determine the timing of each action and line of dialogue, where applicable.

Several different interpretations of the acting may be thumbnailed at this stage, and the most effective one will be used for the scene. Thumbnails are frequently submitted for directorial approval on paper or scanned and timed, sometimes with a dialogue track, on a line tester. This reduces the likelihood of animation corrections later on. Animation thumbnails describe character relationships and amplify emotions and motivations that are only *summarised* on the storyboard. They are *the dress rehearsal for the animated performance*. The function of thumbnails is to capture the animator's thoughts about the characters' feelings and actions in graphic shorthand. They help preserve the animator's spontaneity and inspiration during the sometimes lengthy time it takes to actually animate the scene.

1.3

Major poses
Thumbnail drawings of the major poses in an animated scene block the action and timing before detailed drawings are done.

Figures 1.4, 1.5 and 1.6 show some animation thumbnails I drew for the lion and tiger storyboards in Figure 1.1. Related scenes in a sequence are usually thumbnailed at the same time so that the character performance will remain consistent – or gradually develop over time. *Animated scenes do not exist in isolation.* It is vitally important to know what occurs before and after the scene you are animating since your performance needs to be consistent with the acting in the remainder of the sequence. This is especially important if you are animating scenes out of sequential order. Keep the storyboards on your desk and refer to them often so that you know how each scene fits into the sequence.

Field guides and camera moves are not important at this stage, but variety of scenes adds interest to the story. The animation will most likely be staged a bit wider than the storyboards to allow for character movement. Neither boards nor thumbnails are final artwork. Thumbnails are *always* rough. The drawings can be on one sheet of paper, or on self-stick notes (these are especially useful as they can be easily revised or rearranged).

Feelings hurt, 'what is this?'

Tiger can't see well without glasses, doesn't know it's a log, pulls glasses in from offscreen

Puts glasses on, lowers log offscreen

1

1

I see...

ve-rry funny, guys...

1

1.4

Rough animation thumbnails
The tiger's personality is developed through his movements.

Interpreting the storyboards

In Figure 1.4 I start by writing a brief sentence or two on the paper describing what is going on in the sequence. If there is dialogue, I write it as well. Since this assignment was done without dialogue, I note the tiger's thoughts and emotions (puzzled and a little hurt). In this scene, he nearsightedly tries to view the log and has to fumble for his glasses. He is resigned when the glasses reveal that he has been played for a fool. This action helps define his character.

Thumbnails can indicate timing for separate actions. In Figure 1.5 I added a new drawing (labelled b) after I thumbnailed the main action with the glasses. In Figure 1.6 (on page 18), the tiger tries to laugh the joke off but goes to pieces when the lion grabs the glasses. He reacts submissively, actually crawling at the lion's feet, rather than by defending himself. The sequence has a subtext: *The tiger does not want to fight. He is frightened of the other animals and does not know his own strength.* Often I write the subtext on the thumbnail page as well. Keep the subtext in the back of your mind and you will find that the character acting stays 'in character'. All of the tiger's moves are defensive and ineffectual while the lion moves in a direct, aggressive fashion.

Some of these thumbnails slightly change the staging in the storyboard. For example, I have the tiger look nearsightedly down at the log rather than peer offscreen at the laughing animals as in the storyboard, the better to show his defective vision and timid character.

The scene of the tiger peering offscreen has been eliminated. Of course the director has to approve any acting or cutting changes an animator makes – usually, thumbnail changes are approved when they 'plus' (add to) the story point! (Note: The changes were approved.)

Not every action in a scene needs to be thumbnailed. For example, the lion holding the tiger's glasses (in Scene 4 of Figure 1.6) could pretend to bite them or put them on his own eyes, depending on the time available. One thumbnail for the basic attitude will be enough if the scene is short. I often thumbnail more than one version of the acting and pick the one that suits the story best, exactly the way I thumbnail different camera angles in a storyboard. *I always have the storyboard pinned on the desk while drawing the thumbnails and animating the scenes.*

The animation thumbnails portray the characters' personalities and inner thoughts through movement. Storyboards do not do this; they set the *story*, basic *character acting and attitudes, timing* and *staging.* The animator brings a particular attitude toward the character's performance just as a human actor does. However, an animator is often interpreting a role that is physically impossible for a human actor to perform. No two animators should interpret their characters in precisely the same way. (In a feature film, the character lead or supervising animator determines the character's personality and characteristic actions in test animation scenes after consultation with the directors. Other members of the animation crew will then use the lead's performance as a guide when animating their scenes.)

1.5

An additional drawing
The tiger puts his glasses on and blinks at the camera to show that he can now see, lowering the log offscreen as he does so. He then brings the log back into the shot. This directs the audience's eye to the glasses and makes the story point read better.

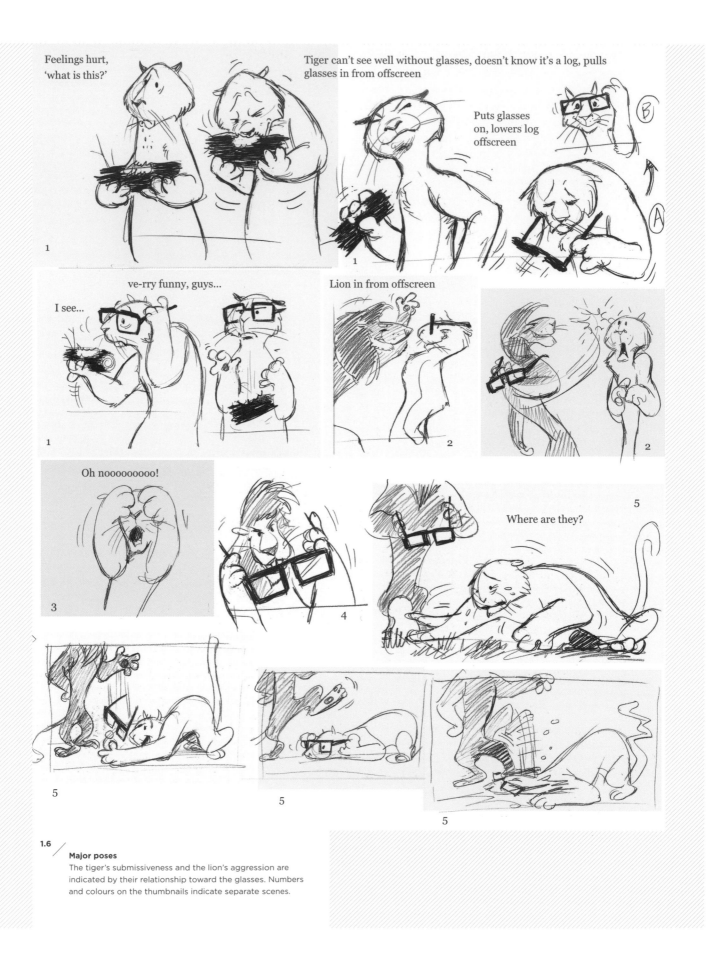

Feelings hurt, 'what is this?'

Tiger can't see well without glasses, doesn't know it's a log, pulls glasses in from offscreen

Puts glasses on, lowers log offscreen

ve-rry funny, guys...

I see...

Lion in from offscreen

Oh noooooooooo!

Where are they?

1.6

Major poses

The tiger's submissiveness and the lion's aggression are indicated by their relationship toward the glasses. Numbers and colours on the thumbnails indicate separate scenes.

Leica/story reels: Timing the performance

One important element that is missing from my animation thumbnails is TIME. The original student storyboards were edited, or *slugged*, to a musical soundtrack that provided timing for the project. Since the story reel (also known as a Leica reel) is not included here, I am 'free timing' the tiger and giving him a lot more to do than his creator originally intended, to illustrate how thumbnails develop from storyboards. But this action would not be possible in the time allocated for the scene. Perhaps the timing of the scenes could be *opened up* (lengthened) if the director approves, but this is unlikely to happen if the project has a set length, for example in a musical number. *Always know how long your sequence and scene is before starting the thumbnails*. There is no point in drawing the tiger fumbling for his glasses if you only have one or two seconds available in the scene. Note that I draw the characters' bodies and avoid tight close-ups. It is important to know where a character's feet and backbone are, even if you are working in medium shot or medium close-up. Always extend your thumbnail and animation drawings 'outside the box' (field guide or screen boundary area) even if your scene is staged as a medium close-up. A scene's fielding is often changed after the animator creates the performance. Your drawings also have more integrity if they relate to the space surrounding them.

TIP

Maintaining consistency

It is better to draw thumbnails *for all scenes in your sequence* at the start of your assignment rather than before each individual scene as it is animated. This method will keep the character acting consistent throughout the sequence even if scenes are animated out of order (which usually happens in production). It also makes it easier to develop the character performance over time. Always keep the original storyboards pinned up for acting and continuity reference while thumbnailing and animating your scenes.

Prioritisation or knowing your 'A-B-Cs'

Thumbnails allow an animator to set the scene priorities before beginning animation since they allow you to see which scenes have the most elaborate action and acting. An 'A' scene is one that is vital to the storyline and usually contains the most complicated animation. A 'B' scene is still important to the storyline but may be a simple one-character shot rather than a two-shot with dialogue. Since it will take less time to animate than an 'A', it will take second priority in production. A 'C' scene has lowest priority and may be eliminated if the limitations of time and budget intervene in the production, as they often do. 'C' scenes may still be necessary for the story but they can easily be modified or shortened if required. (A background with a held level is a good example of a 'C' scene. Crowd scenes are also usually 'C' scenes.) In Figure 1.6, Scene 5 (where the tiger crawls on the ground looking for the glasses only to have them broken by the lion) is an 'A' scene and should be animated first.

All the other scenes, except for Scene 1, are 'B' scenes. The puzzled tiger fumbling with the log may be amusing to watch, but *Scene 1 is a 'C' scene*. Even though it should not be cut entirely out of the picture, it may be shortened and the action simplified so that he merely puts on the glasses. This change will not affect the basic story. Why do we do this? Animators have the most time and energy at the beginning of a production. If the most important and complicated scenes are done first, they will be done (and done *well*) when the animation is completed. A simple 'C' scene done at the end of the production will not take too much of the animator's by-now-depleted time and energy, or it may be cut without leaving a hole in the film.

Next >

Next, we will discuss how all animation works out of a story context.

Good actors:
Designs that animate

'Any pose you think of, you must draw with facility, so that it isn't what the pose is so much as why is it being drawn – what emotion is being expressed.'

– Shamus Culhane, *Animation: From Script to Screen*

Developing a story context for your animation

The previous section shows how storyboards inspire character animators to create a performance within a story context. What if you are a student learning to animate walk cycles or express the character's emotions? Your scene is a self-contained assignment; it is not part of a longer film. How do you show the character's personality? More importantly, how do you avoid the pitfalls of clichéd poses and movements that can make your scene resemble a thousand others?

This question has a simple answer. *All* animation is performed within a story context. It all depends on how you define 'story'. The story must be simplified to meet the criteria of your assignment. Instead of a three-act feature treatment, or even a three-sentence outline for a short film, your 'story' can be the character's mental state, a relationship between two characters, or the interaction of a character and an object. *Your* object in each instance is to show a pantomimic impression of the character's inner feelings – *why* it moves as well as *how*. Your emotional interpretation will be different from the next person's if you use YOUR emotions and do not imitate those of others in animated films or animated textbooks.

The animated character, like a human actor, does not stand alone. It is influenced by its background and its relationship with other elements in the scene.

This is where animated acting begins.

An exercise figure

Take a look at the simple humanoid character shown in Figure 1.7: it contains no design details such as hair or clothing that could determine age, sex or cultural context. The figure (let's call it Sam, a name that can be used for male and female characters) is a blank slate that has been used to demonstrate animation exercises in a variety of books and is also available as a rigged CGI figure. It has no determining characteristics – it can be young or old, male or female.

Sam is easy to draw, but is not particularly interesting. In the words of Børge Ring, 'You must *make* it interesting!'

So we will follow Børge Ring's advice. In Figure 1.8, I give Sam a *prop* to work with.

1.7

A simple humanoid figure
This humanoid figure is simple to draw, and offers a blank slate for the animator to develop into a character.

1.8

A prop
A ball is a basic prop used in many beginning exercises for animation.

1.1 Character acting with a prop

My animation students perform this exercise to warm-up every time class meets. It's a wonderful way to get the creative juices flowing. The basic 'emotional' acting exercise was devised by Shamus Culhane in his classic book <u>Animation: From Script to Screen</u>, using elf characters that had predetermined personalities and designs that set them into a specific context. I've extensively modified the exercise, which led to some extensive criticism from Shamus (more about that later).

Let's get started.

An animated ball can be a simple prop, or it can be another character in your scene. We will thumbnail Sam reacting to and with the ball in a variety of attitudes.

➺ Do not use close-ups and do not rely on facial expressions. Use full figure drawings and total-body acting.

➺ First, list some emotions and attitudes on a piece of paper; try these first, then add your own later on:

Anger; love or joy; greed; boredom; curiosity and finally sickness.

1.9

Thumbnails are always 'rough'
Show construction lines and don't be afraid to draw fast and rough.

➺ Draw a line on the paper for a floor plane, but do not add background details at this time.

➺ Sketch Sam with the ball in full figure for each emotion. Draw a few rough poses that express his inner feelings; don't only do one. Each emotion may be done as a separate exercise on a different sheet of paper. Work with the body attitudes first; the facial expressions are not as important.

➺ **Time your exercise.** Start with five minutes' drawing time for the first emotion; then try decreasing the timing for each subsequent one. You will eventually find that a minute is enough time to draw two or three thumbnails for one emotion.

➺ Make these sketches **quick** and **rough**. Do not worry about clean lines; scribbles are fine as long as the poses read.

➺ Construct the figure as you would a gesture drawing. Portraying the action is more important than creating a finished, 'clean' drawing. Get the line of action and body mass first, then rough in where the feet will be, and **draw through** the torso so that arms and legs attach convincingly on opposite sides of the body. Thumbnails do not need to be 'pretty' – just pretty effective at conveying the gesture.

➺ Do not erase drawings and do not cross any out; keep them all. Start a new sketch on the same page if the old one is not pleasing to you.

➺ Write the corresponding emotions underneath each sketch. You can also include a short description of Sam's thoughts as I have done in Figure 1.10. (I've drawn all the emotions on one page; please do yours separately, and do more than one sketch for each emotion.)

➺ Do not make the sketches too large. Two or three should fit on a sheet of notebook paper. Make sure the character doesn't go off the page.

➺ When you have finished this exercise, turn the drawings over and view them lit from below on a light box or animation desk. (You can reverse them in a computer graphics program if you are working digitally.)

➼ This technique gives you a different perspective on the drawings and shows you the areas that work and those that do not.

➼ After you have done this, redraw and improve the poses, working to the same timing as before, **on the reverse side of the sketch** and once again write the emotions underneath the drawings. Label the revised drawings Version 2.

➼ Shade both versions in black so that they read as pure silhouette. Which sketches read best?

➼ Version 2 will often be superior to Version 1, since you can see the weak areas in your original drawings when you view them in reverse. This enables you to **push** or strengthen the attitudes in Version 2 so that silhouettes and acting read better.

➼ Date your sketches and keep them in a folder. Repeat the exercise on a daily (or per-class) basis, returning to the same emotions a few weeks apart. See how your later versions compare with your early ones.

Note: Shamus Culhane made the astute criticism that this exercise didn't **'use the characters that you are animating'**. Try doing the assignment using a **simple** character of your own instead of Sam (don't use pre-existing animated characters that already have 'set' personalities). Your character's personality now influences your choice of pose.

Happy ('Would you be mine?')

Curious ('Is this mine?')

Greed ('It's MINE!')

Anger ('THIS ISN'T MINE!')

Sad ('This cannot be mine')

1.10

Developing a personality
A character with no obvious characteristics starts to develop a personality through his body attitudes and mental relationship toward an object.

1.2 Exercises with attitude

Now animate a walk cycle with the character in **one** of the 'attitudes'. An angry walk will differ considerably from a happy or depressed one. Use Sam or use your own character – but keep it **in** character.

Next, animate the character throwing a ball in a scene running ten seconds or less. You may use the same attitude or choose one of the others. Write the attitude/emotion on the top of your new thumbnail sheet for the scene. Draw thumbnails of the major keys or action poses and make sure that every pose depicts your chosen emotion. (Do not change emotions in mid-scene; we will get to that later.) An angry character will walk angrily up to the ball, pick it up, and throw it angrily – possibly through a window. A loving or happy character might gently play catch with the ball, a depressed one might not bother to pick it up, and the greedy one might not want to throw it to anyone else, ever! Find your own way of expressing the character's thought processes through its action. There is no 'one' correct way to animate this assignment just as there is no 'one' way of interpreting a Shakespearean role.

CGI (Computer-Generated Imagery) animators draw thumbnails before beginning to animate just as cartoon animators do. There are programs available that let you import your thumbnails into the scene or draw them directly on the monitor so that the model may match the pose. When I visited Pixar Animation Studios a few years ago, I asked John Lasseter, Brad Bird, Joe Ranft, and Jean Pinkava whether they still drew thumbnails before beginning their animation. The answer came in a roar: **'HELL, YES!'**

There will always be differences in how the eye perceives animation in the two media since CGI works with **solid shapes**, while hand-drawn animation is **linear**. A hand-drawn character will seem to move faster than a fully modelled CGI character even when the scene timings are exactly the same.

TIP

Design changes

You may find that your own character does not portray some emotions in this exercise as easily as Sam does. This may be due to the basic design, which might contain too much 'pencil mileage' – details that can obstruct clear poses or take too much time to draw. (There is a reason why Sam has no clothing, hair, or other distinguishing marks!) It is normal for animated characters' designs to be reworked once they have been tested in motion. At the Walt Disney Animation studio, character model sheets were never finalised until an entire scene of test animation was produced and keys from that scene were often used for the action model sheet. If you find that some details on the character interfere with a pose, try leaving them off and working for good silhouette value. Then revise the character designs, using some of the 'acting' poses as rough model guides. The result will be a stronger design and a character that is easier to animate.

Angry Sam throws ball – or not!

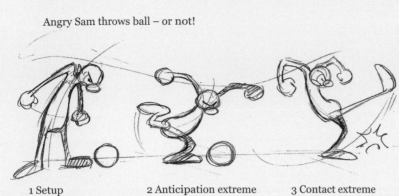
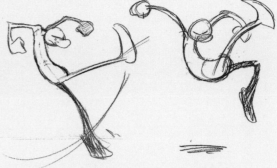

1 Setup

2 Anticipation extreme

3 Contact extreme

3a and 3b are breakdowns that go even farther than the contact extreme

4 and 5 are breakdowns showing overlapping action as body parts move at different rates

6 is recovery

7 cushions into final pose 8

1.11

Different performances
Sam performs a simple 'ball toss' differently, depending on his/her attitude toward the ball.

1.12

CGI
A CGI ape performs the exercise differently to a hand-drawn character, but the same thought processes are used for the animated performance.
Character design, rig, and poses © 2008 by Ignacio Barrios

Next >

Next, we will learn how dialogue animation was handled in the past and how techniques have changed today.

An introduction to dialogue animation

Caricature (n.) a picture, description, or imitation of a person in which certain striking characteristics are exaggerated in order to create a comic or grotesque effect.

Character actors

It has been said that a good voice actor can create 50 per cent of the animated performance. This is particularly evident when an animated character is designed as a caricature of the actor who provides the voice. It is a relatively simple matter to analyse the actor's characteristic movements and incorporate a caricatured version into the animated character's performance. Many excellent animated characters have done this very thing.

The drawback to this system is that the caricatured references may not remain relevant as the film ages. If the original performance is good, this should not create a problem. The caricature of Rowan Atkinson as Zazu the Hornbill in *The Lion King* (1994) is amusing, but the caricature is not essential to the performance; Zazu will remain amusing even if the audience is not familiar with the actor's other work.

Then there are occasional instances where a nondescript or ordinary voice track does not provide any obvious reference points for the animator. I once worked with a famous actor at the end of their career when their voice was not at its best. I had the character moving in an even sprightlier manner than usual to cover the fact that the voice track was not particularly strong. The animation helped the voice acting, rather than the other way around.

TIP

Caricature

Some animated performances incorporate the caricatured appearance and movements of the voice actor. You should not rely too much on pop culture references since the passage of time and cultural shifts will often date them. British audiences got the 'in-joke' of Rowan Atkinson's avian caricature, but the actor was relatively unknown in the USA when *The Lion King* was made. Zazu the character was amusing even without this knowledge.

1.13

Rowan Atkinson and Zazu the Hornbill
Rowan Atkinson was the voice for Zazu the Hornbill in *The Lion
King* and his large facial features were caricatured in the bird's
design. The voice actor may also provide reference for the physical
appearance and characteristic mannerisms and movements of an
animated character.
The Lion King © Disney Enterprises, Inc. *Four Weddings and a Funeral* ©
Polygram/Channel 4/Working Title/The Kobal Collection.

Mouthing off:
Full body acting and dialogue animation

When sound film became the standard in the late 1920s there was a lengthy period of trial and error where animators attempted different methods of portraying mouth movement for dialogue scenes. The Max Fleischer Studio usually *post-synched* their dialogue to the animation. Jack Mercer and Mae Questel would ad-lib Popeye the Sailor and Olive Oyl's amusing voice tracks after the film had actually been animated – and the characters' mouths did not move. Other cartoons from this period tended to feature over-analysed, carefully pronounced dialogue that bore little or no resemblance to actual human speech. Mouth movement was seen as *primary*, or *the most important* action in a dialogue scene. Each mouth shape was treated as a separate design and drawn in laborious detail. As a result every mouth shape was *emphasised equally* and handled independently from the body action, which led to grotesque facial distortions (see Figure 1.14).

Animated performance took a quantum leap forward when animators at the Walt Disney Studio discovered that dialogue animation was in fact *secondary action*, and that dialogue delivery was 'put over' by body movement and attitudes rather than over-analysed mouth shapes.

The change is apparent in a specific scene in an early Mickey Mouse cartoon. In *The Delivery Boy* (1931) Minnie Mouse flirts with Mickey Mouse in front of an upright piano. 'Go on and *play* something', she says winningly while leaning over the side of the piano. Mickey inhales deeply and replies, '…I have to be *coaxed!*' – and his awkward, knock-kneed pose perfectly portrays his amused shyness. Minnie walks up to him with a feminine swing of her hips and bats her eyes as she says, 'Well… I'm coaxin' ya!' Both characters' movements are naturalistic and beautifully timed to the dialogue. The body action is used to create the character performances. The mouth shapes are underplayed and were clearly added after the action was blocked in. The dialogue in the rest of the film is handled in a more standard fashion. Surprisingly, over-animated mouths continued to be produced well after *The Delivery Boy* was made. It took more trial and error before the animators learned to let the body movement carry the bulk of the acting. (*The Delivery Boy* can be viewed on *The Walt Disney Treasures: Mickey Mouse in Black And White volume 1* DVD.)

The Disney animators began to animate body action first in dialogue scenes, using the soundtrack as a rough timing aid. Mouths would be added later after the character acting was approved. This approach eliminated the over-animated 1920s mouths and made the performances more believable and naturalistic. Fleischer Studios animator Shamus Culhane retrained at Disney to learn the new animation techniques. Here is his description of what happened when he and fellow animator Al Eugster returned to Fleischer's in the mid-1930s.

'...there was no satisfactory interpretation of dialogue (in animation) until it was discovered at Disney's that there was a definite need for body English. The louder the volume, the more violent the effort of the body to produce it. The size of the mouth was a very minor contribution to the end result... [At the Fleischer studio] ex-Disney animator Al Eugster roughed out a scene for *Gulliver's Travels* (1939) and, following the Disney technique, omitted the mouths. They would be added later if the body movements were in sync. Dave Fleischer, the producer, commented on the accuracy of the mouth action during a sweatbox session. When he was told that there were no mouths, he couldn't believe it. The synch was perfect. He was mystified when the scene was projected again and he saw that indeed there were no mouths.'

– Shamus Culhane, *Animation: From Script to Screen*

Curiously enough, some animation textbooks provided very limited analysis of dialogue animation. In one instance, the dialogue mouths were taken from a film where a character shouted the line – so each mouth shape was as distorted and overdone as the 1920s 'over-analysed' animation, though the drawing was considerably better.

1.14

Exaggerated dialogue
1920s dialogue animation was a technical exercise that did not relate to design volume or body action.

1.15

No need to shout
You don't shout every time you speak, and neither should your animated character. Mouth shapes will vary in intensity depending on the character's emotion and the voice actor's performance. There are no 'standard mouth shapes' for dialogue animation.

Found in translation: Non-standard lip-synch

Human beings' mouth shapes vary by nationality, language background, or physiology. Stanley Kubrick's movie *Dr Strangelove or: How I Learned to Stop Worrying and Love the Bomb* (1964) featured a gallery of human cartoons, three of them played by the same actor. The brilliant Peter Sellers used a 'stiff upper lip' for his British captain, a mush-mouth accent for his American President, and a permanent death-grin for the Nazi scientist Dr Strangelove. Sellers pronounced all of Strangelove's phonetics except for 'P', 'B' and 'M' through tightly clenched teeth. On the other hand cowboy actor Slim Pickens seemed to pronounce every word with his mouth open wide, revealing every one of his teeth.

There is no *one* way to perform animation dialogue, no more than there is only *one* way to animate a character. Not only will no two characters speak alike in good animation – the same character may use different mouth shapes at different times, depending on the situation or the mood. A dialogue track breakdown should reflect changes in emotion and emphasis. Animators can add their own emphases after listening to the soundtrack – this becomes even more important when computer programs that utilise 'standard' mouth shapes are used for track breakdowns. Non-English speakers may use different phonetics, as shown in the track breakdown in Figure 1.16.

1.16

French phonetics

A Francophone will 'hear' English sounds differently than a native speaker. French phonetics in the soundtrack breakdown can help a non-English speaking animator use the correct mouth shapes for English lip synch. (French phonetics by Natalie Garceau-Turner).

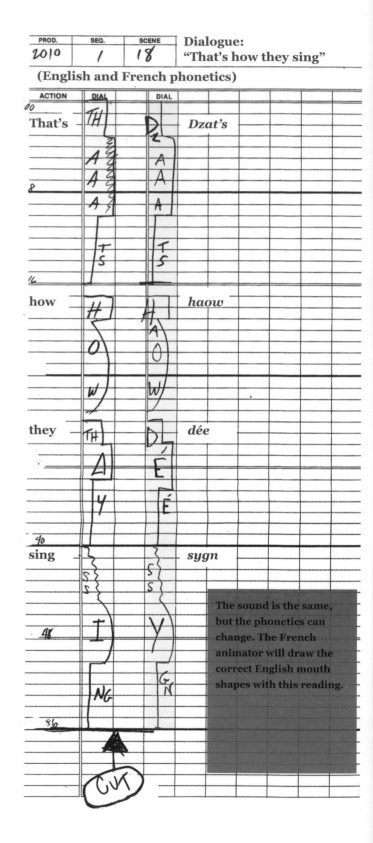

PROD.	SEQ.	SCENE	Dialogue:
2010	1	18	"That's how they sing"

(English and French phonetics)

The sound is the same, but the phonetics can change. The French animator will draw the correct English mouth shapes with this reading.

c

Of course, the whole point of a Doomsday Machine is lost, if you *keep* it a secret!

b

Shoot, a fella could have a pretty good weekend in Vegas with all that stuff.

a

Condition red, sir. Yes. Jolly good idea, keeps the men on their toes.

1.17

Dr Strangelove

The characters in *Dr Strangelove* used exaggerated mouth shapes which gave the film a cartoon quality. Peter Sellers' British captain (a) spoke with a 'stiff upper lip'. Slim Pickens' cowboy pilot (b) opened his mouth wide for each word. While Dr Strangelove (c), also played by Peter Sellers, hissed each line through tightly clenched teeth.

1.3 Body attitude and dialogue

Let us explore some variations on dialogue full-body acting, once again using Sam as the example. Take some of the sketches you developed for the emotional acting in Exercise 1.2. Choose one drawing for each emotion: **Anger; love or joy; greed; boredom; curiosity and sickness.**

Next, write the dialogue 'I love you' underneath each drawing, as if the character was **saying the line in each particular mood or attitude**. Now, choose one of the emotions and draw a series of thumbnails showing Sam throwing the ball while saying 'I love you' – keeping the emotional attitude consistent throughout the scene. You may draw mouths, but concentrate mainly on the body attitudes. Sam may address an offscreen character, or talk to the ball – it's all possible in animation! The dialogue may be broken up into separate words that appear under more than one sketch. This helps time the action even before the soundtrack has been recorded. (Character drawings and storyboards are often shown to voice actors during a recording session to give them an idea of the director's desired reading for the line.)

I   LOVE YOU!

I   love you

1.18

Dialogue
The dialogue is written under the thumbnails where Sam will actually be speaking. Note how the spacing of the words indicates the timing of the line reading, even when a track is not present.

a

I LOVE you

I love you!

I LOVE YOU!

I love you?

I...love...you...

I love you

b

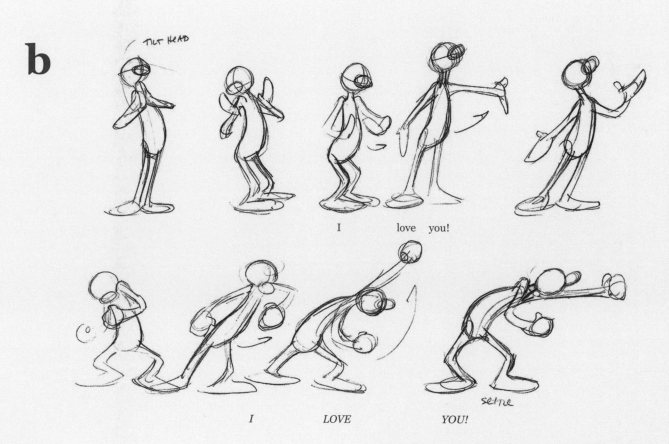

TILT HEAD

I   love   you!

I   LOVE   YOU!

1.19

Body attitude

First sketch attitudes for the scene, choose the best one or two (a) and then thumbnail the animation keys, writing the dialogue underneath the drawings (b). Try different interpretations and don't worry about changes – this is when it's easiest to make them! Work rough and concentrate on body attitudes. Shoot a pose test with the rough – *don't worry about the mouths*. The dialogue should work with the body action. Add mouths **last**. Note that the same dialogue may be emphasised or timed differently depending on the character's emotion or attitude.

1	2	3	4	5	6	7
I	love	you	more	than I	can	say

1.20

Over-animated action

Every word and pose in this scene is equally emphasised,
resulting in frantic and over-animated action that confuses
and tires the viewer.

Coining a phrase: Pacing animated dialogue

Remember that animation acting is *movement
with a purpose.*

A common animation error is to have the
character changing body attitudes so often that
there is literally a new pose for each new word.
This can be very tiring to watch since poses that
are equally emphasised will cancel each other
out.

This animation portrays frantic and meaningless
motion rather than a controlled, nuanced
performance (see Figure 1.20).

Of course there are always exceptions to the rule.
My first animation of Max in *A Goofy Movie* (1995)
has a new pose for each word of dialogue – or
does it? In this case, the mouth action is only
incidental to the scene and his repeated leaps
are variations on two poses (see Figure 1.21).
Max has overslept and is impatient with his friend
P. J. The frantic action emphasises his
nervousness and anger. The dialogue was used
to time his actions, but it is definitely secondary
action – indeed, much of this line does not appear
in the final picture.

Animated dialogue is best performed by using
key poses for dialogue *phrases*, rather than
for individual words. This is why the system of
blocking body action first and adding the mouths
later works so well. Fewer, well chosen poses lead
to clearer action.

Phrasing the action means that key poses
will change in relation to a sentence, or partial
sentence, rather than to individual words. Two
basic attitudes might be all that is needed for
a scene; body action moves between them,
and secondary action on head, arms, and mouth
combines with facial expression to vary the
timing and minimise the chance of 'floating
(directionless, evenly timed) animation'.
A 'moving hold' also keeps the animation
from popping abruptly between key poses.

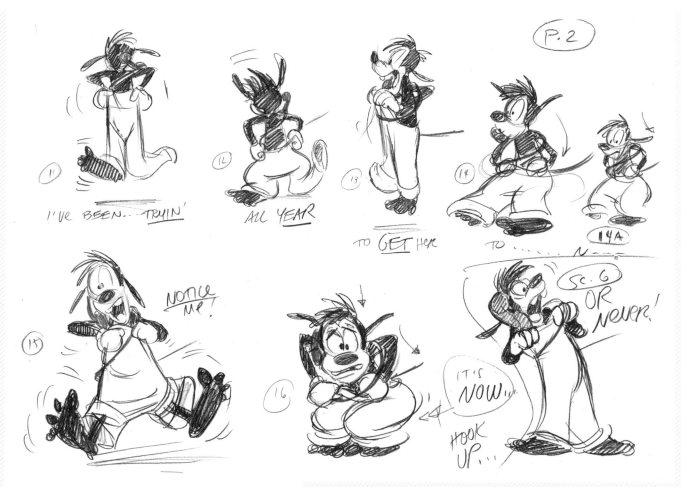

Secondary action

Max's unpreparedness and impatience with his friend
is reflected in his frantic movements. The mouth action
is secondary to the body movement.

Thumbnails by Nancy Beiman, *A Goofy Movie*

© Disney Enterprises, Inc.

Stillness in motion: The moving hold

Moving holds keep the action fluid and leave the strongest poses or holds for the greatest emotional impact. Different parts of the figure move at different times so that the 'jumping jack' quality of the poses in Fig. 1.20 is eliminated. *Phrasing also should be used in your lip-synch animation.* Do not try to laboriously draw every mouth shape. Draw phonetics for the major sounds, then breakdown mouths where necessary. Leave inbetweens for last, when you are inbetweening the rest of the scene. The lip-synch will work if the body attitudes are working.

1   2   3

I **love** you   more than   I can **say**

1.22

Phrasing
Dialogue works better when it is 'phrased'. This moving hold underplays the animation and moves between two poses to keep the character 'alive', emphasising the acting and the strong emotion in the dialogue.

DVD reference: Dialogue analysis

The Jungle Book (1967) has some of the finest dialogue animation that the Walt Disney animation studio ever produced. Human, ape, cat, snake and bear characters show a variety of different mouth shapes. Two excellent sequences to view occur just after the famous song 'I Wanna Be Like You'. In the first sequence, Bagheera tells Baloo that he must take Mowgli back to the Man Village. In the next sequence, Baloo breaks the news to Mowgli, who runs off in anger.

Run the sequences with the original English track. Then turn off the sound and watch them silent. Analyse the body acting, the emotions conveyed, and the use of props. (Baloo gets *a lot* of mileage out of a bunch of grapes.) The story point is conveyed without the soundtrack. Watch Baloo's acting change as he learns of the danger that Mowgli faces. Now, switch tracks to each of the other languages in the 'setup' screen and watch the sequences with each new language track. The synchronisation will still be perfect since the mouth shapes are phonetics only (and the French and Spanish dialogue is cleverly written to synchronise with open mouth shapes in the English-language animation).

Dr Strangelove, or: How I Learned to Stop Worrying and Love the Bomb (1964) has brilliantly cartoonish performances by Peter Sellers, George C. Scott, Slim Pickens and Sterling Hayden. Note the use of props: Sellers uses cigarettes, Hayden uses a cigar, and Scott says all his lines with a mouthful of chewing gum.

One of my student films had numerous scenes where the character shot its head up, reacted down slightly, and held its body completely still as the hair and whiskers then animated or overlapped up. (This is a common error in student animation.) Animator Frank Thomas suggested that the majority of my holds be 'moving'. Pure holds, he said, should be reserved for the most important poses or an emphasis in the action. In other words, a moving hold is a comma and a straight hold is a period or full stop in animated film grammar. Imagine. If. Every. Sentence. Was. Like. This. It's far better, really, to vary our punctuation.

a

b

1.23

Secondary action

Figure a shows animation that pops right into a hold with
secondary action overlapping – figure b 'phrases' the action
better so that the character is in a moving hold until the final
held pose. This varies the timing and improves the acting.

1.4 Transitions between attitudes

Here is a line of dialogue that transitions between two character attitudes. Since we do not have a recorded track, we will imagine how an actor might read the line. The first step, whether or not the track is present, is to underline the words that we wish to emphasise in animation.

'**I love you**, but I wish you wouldn't keep **forgetting to tighten the cap** on the peanut butter jar.'

Next, record the dialogue, directing the actor to emphasise the words you have underlined in the 'script'. You may wish to experiment by having the actor read the line with different emphases, which will possibly change the animated performance. Choose the best take and break down the track into phonetics. Now the voice track sets the tone and timing for the scene. The character also gets to work with a prop, which is desirable in a dialogue scene. There is nothing more uninteresting in animation than lengthy shots of talking heads. **Always find something for your characters to do while they are talking.**

It is now time to 'perform' the scene.

➤ First: **Listen to the track!** Write the dialogue at the top of the page, underlining the words that are emphasised.

➤ Write the **point** of the scene just beneath the line. Use one sentence. Don't try to say too much! Two examples: '**I am becoming increasingly exasperated at the behaviour of my significant other.**' or '**I love my significant other in spite of what he/she just did.**' This will keep your acting consistent and provide a 'story' for this exercise.

➤ Write the emotions that the line suggests to you just underneath the 'point'. You may think of more than one variation.

➤ Next, draw several thumbnails using these emotions as a guide for your poses. Draw more than one set if you have more than one interpretation of the line.

➤ Write the dialogue under the thumbnails, breaking up the sentences so that the words help time the action. You may also write the emotional state under some thumbnails to indicate where emotional transitions take place.

➤ Choose the best thumbnail interpretation for your scene and begin to animate. First, draw or set the key poses on the body only – without the mouths.

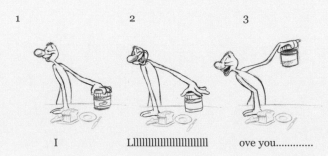

1   2   3

I   Llllllllllllllllllllllllllll   ove you.............

4   5   6

(moving hold)

➤ Shoot a line test with the recorded soundtrack, holding the keys for as long as needed. Adjust timing where necessary. Add your breakdowns on the body, but do not include mouths.

➤ Shoot another test. Adjust the timing on the keys and breakdowns so that the body action works well with the track.

➤ Then, and ONLY then, draw or set the mouth's key poses on the body's keys and breakdowns. The mouth's extreme shapes might not match up with the extremes on the body! An extreme mouth position may occur on a 'body' breakdown. Chart the timing for the mouths separately from the body charts if this is the case. **Dialogue synchronisation mouth shapes always occur on the <u>exact</u> frame of the sound or on the frame before, but the body accents usually hit four frames before the vocal emphasis.**

➤ Inbetween your scene. The mouth shapes may also be inbetweens at this point, but look at your track reading and listen to the track again to be sure!

Different character attitudes will change the acting. Sam may be too much in love with the 'other' to even notice where the peanut butter is being applied.

Note: I don't recommend physically acting out your scenes for reasons that I will discuss later – but sticky peanut butter is one reason not to do it! **Draw what you know and feel.** Act out the scene through your thumbnails.

I have given this assignment in animation classes and no two students perform the exercise in precisely the same way. And Sam is just a 'nobody' without an obvious personality. What variations in acting might come when we use more complex characters and dialogue? This topic will be addressed in later chapters.

7	8	9
But	I wish	that you

10	11	12
wouldn't keep	forgetting to tighten	the cap on the peanut butter jar!

1.24

Rough thumbnails
Rough thumbnails should be blocked after you determine the scene point and relevant emotions. *Sam is too much in love to notice that he is making a mess. Emotions: 'Goofily romantic, oblivious.'*

2

Setting the stage: Character and story context

In this chapter you will learn how animation acting will vary depending on the story, and why all animation – even animation exercises – takes place within a story context. There is a description of how a character's internal feelings may influence its external appearance, and of animator Art Babbitt's thought processes when developing a character's personality for short films and commercials.

In the second section you will see how the animator's goal is to create the 'feel' of an action rather than a literal interpretation. You will learn how this may be achieved with the aid of a sketchbook and also see how action sketches from life can be the inspiration for the animation of fantastic creatures. The last part of the chapter discusses common errors in animating large or heavy characters and how a character's weight and volume may influence its acting.

Princess Bland and her Animal Friends
A one-note character's personality is consistent and
its reactions are predictable. Secondary characters may
steal the show from the 'star'.

Don't just *do* something...

'He is willing to help anyone and offers his assistance even when he is not needed and just creates confusion.... Each object or piece of mechanism which to us is lifeless, has a soul and personality in the mind of the Goof. The improbable becomes real where the Goof is concerned.'

– Art Babbitt, 'Analysis of the Goof'. Excerpts from *The Illusion of Life: Disney Animation* by Frank Thomas and Ollie Johnston published by Disney Editions are copyrighted by Disney Enterprises, Inc. and are used by permission from Disney Enterprises, Inc.

You're going out a cartoon but you're coming back a star!

A good animated actor has a depth of personality that sets it apart from the other creatures in the crowd. It appears to think for itself (even if its thought processes might be a bit on the slow side) and it is capable of expressing a variety of emotions that are believable to the audience. As Art Babbitt explained to me:

Q: Is there any sort of a process, when you have a character that has just been designed, of developing its personality and deciding how you will make it move?

Art Babbitt: Well, in 1934, I think it was, I was obliged to establish a character – a personality – for Goofy. Goofy had been one of a crowd in the barnyard – you know, sort of a nondescript character. But I had to find a 'handle'; something to hang onto. So I wrote a thesis [character study] on Goofy, not only describing his physical appearance, but giving some indication of his mental processes.

Q: You did this before you had actually animated the character?

Art Babbitt: That's right.... I think that such a bit of research should be done on all important characters.

– Art Babbitt, interview with Nancy Beiman (1979)

Characters that are only able to express one or two emotions convincingly are known as *one-note* characters because their personalities and their reactions to a given situation are consistent and predictable. One-note characters may be well designed, easy to animate, and very amusing in a short film, but they cannot sustain the audience's interest for a feature-length film. The one-note hero of a feature film may be upstaged by secondary characters that show more emotional variety than the nominal star.

Goofy actually started off as a 'one-note' character in the early Mickey Mouse cartoons. The only thing that distinguished him from the other barnyard characters was his amusing laugh, which was performed by story man Pinto Colvig. Art Babbitt's 1934 essay described Goofy as a likable, honest and kind-hearted soul who knew that he wasn't very bright. Babbitt's character study is a remarkable document that was still in use in 1993 when *A Goofy Movie*, the first feature film 'starring' Goofy, went into production. The animators had Goofy express a variety of

2.1

Goofy

Goofy could portray serious and comic emotions, sometimes simultaneously. In this scene, Goofy makes a bad situation worse by trying to speak 'man to man' with his son at the worst possible time. The prop (a picture of Roxanne, whom Max secretly loves) is essential to the acting performance. Goofy's attitudes express fondness and subtle concern while Max is embarrassed and enraged.

Thumbnails and animation by Nancy Beiman.

A Goofy Movie © Disney Enterprises, Inc.

convincing emotions in the film, and Bill Farmer's fine voice track helped make the character's serious moods as believable as the comic ones.

Why was Goofy a good dramatic actor? For one thing, he has always been portrayed as a bit older than the other classic Disney characters. Mickey Mouse's personality is that of a young boy filled with the spirit of adventure. Donald Duck was a naughty child in his earliest incarnations and a naughty adult in later ones. But Goofy was an adult who displayed the literal-mindedness and 'magical thinking' of a child. It was Goofy (animated by Art Babbitt) who had a battle with a malevolent, seemingly alive piano in *Moving Day* (1936). Donald's explosive temper was displayed in a fight with a fishbowl in the same picture, but the fishbowl was always a prop. Donald, unlike Goofy, did not treat the inanimate object as a living opponent. This reflects the difference in the characters' thought processes.

Goofy is a pretty exceptional character since the personality set in Art Babbitt's essay remained largely consistent for the next 70 years. The Warner Brothers animation studio's characters, on the other hand, went through many 'evolutions'. Their personalities and appearance changed not only over time, but also in cartoons produced by different directors. Compare an early Bugs Bunny cartoon such as *Tortoise Beats Hare* (Tex Avery, 1941) in which an aggressive Bugs races a clever turtle named Cecil and repeatedly loses, with the later *Baby Buggy Bunny* (Chuck Jones, 1954) where a compassionate Bugs 'adopts' a poor little orphan who is actually an escaped bank robber dressed as a baby. Bugs is just as aggressive in the Jones film, but only after the 'baby' attacks him. Trial and error showed the Warner animators that Bugs simply could not be the aggressor; he always had to react to provocation.

The long and the short of it

Long-form animators can develop their characters' personalities over time, whether during the several years of a feature film's production or during decades of short cartoons 'starring' characters such as Bugs Bunny. Characters also evolve over the course of a long-running television series such as *The Simpsons*.

On the other hand, short-form animation may have only a minute or so available to tell a story. I asked Art Babbitt how one managed to create a character in a very short film:

Q: It struck me that all the character development research you mentioned was originally intended for features and theatrical shorts [see page 42]. How would you go about establishing a character in a 30-second or one-minute film?

Art Babbitt: Well, you'd be surprised how often that happens. For instance, in a one-minute commercial I did for Snowdrift Shortening in the middle fifties [it won a New York Art Director's prize in 1956], there was a wife and husband involved. The husband was a crotchety guy. I arrived at that after thinking it over. The woman was trying to please him, but when she wanted something she *wheedled* it out of him, rather than coming right out and asking for it.

> " You analyse the character beforehand. Yet, as you work with the character, you discover other facets that were not evident originally. The character becomes richer and richer as the time goes on, not only internally, but externally, too. There are certain things that grow with the passage of time.
>
> – Art Babbitt interview with Nancy Beiman (1979) "

The husband was more forceful, and the woman was obliging him. *You think not only of their internal character... but of their appearance.* They were a middle-aged couple. *How would the [internal feelings] affect their look?* Especially if you didn't want them to look like the typical cartoon models that you get.

– Interview with Nancy Beiman (1979)

Director/producer John Hubley and animator/designer Art Babbitt designed characters for *John and Marsha*, a 60-second commercial for Snowdrift Shortening, using a modified version of comedian Stan Freberg's famous comedy routine. Freberg reduces often complex soap opera plots to their absolute minimum. His script contains only two words – 'John' and 'Marsha'. Frame 1 introduces us to the characters. We are in a simply furnished dining room. Marsha is a pear-shaped housewife wearing a modest dress and little jewellery. John is an overweight man in his fifties who wears a 'comb-over' that symbolises false dignity and pride. John's head is high. All's right with the world and he's the king of his castle. Marsha is in the servile 'wheedling' pose that Babbitt describes in the interview. She submits a cake for John's approval.

In Frame 2, the much-too-heavy cake has definitely failed to please John. He angrily and dramatically accuses Marsha, who does not yet understand how she has offended him.

In Frame 3 John is still in his accusatory pose (note the moving hold!) as Marsha runs crying from the room. John's over-the-top reaction to a simple problem implies something going on behind the scenes: it is clear that he is never pleased with *anything* Marsha does. The man is a brute. This isn't about the cake. The poor woman's marriage is toast.

All of this is clearly expressed with only two words of dialogue and superb character animation.

After a short cutaway to Marsha's mother, who recommends 'Snowdrift' and a brief sequence where Marsha bakes a new cake using the product, we return to the dining room where John sits fuming in Frame 4. Everything about his body language depicts repressed rage making his monosyllabic reply simultaneously dramatic and funny.

2.2

Snowdrift: John and Marsha
The character relationships change depending on the way John and Marsha pronounce one another's names, and an entire story of love, rejection, and atonement is depicted in one minute. In the commercial, John and Marsha's ordinary appearance provides an ironic counterpoint to the passionate dialogue.

Marsha is servile as before in Frame 4, then more confident as she offers John the cake in Frame 5. John's horrified reaction in Frames 5 and 6 invokes the subtext of the ruined marriage and the soap opera theme: Will John get his dessert, or is he about to get his *just deserts*? Marsha stands triumphant in Frame 7 as the new feather-light cake floats to the table. John approves of the new treat. John and Marsha reach for one another as equals in Frame 8 and go into a torrid embrace in Frame 9. John passionately declaims 'MARSHA!' one last time in Frame 10 and draws a curtain on the scene. Marsha's giggling tells us what is going on behind the curtain as the announcer's voice-over calmly describes the product. (The chair that appears under Marsha's back in Frame 9 is a perfect example of subliminal suggestion.)

The passion and emotion of a much longer film has been elegantly depicted in 60 seconds of brilliant animation produced to a short deadline.

It is unlikely that Art Babbitt acted out any of the movements of his characters. As he stated, the stylised acting in this cartoon reflects the characters' thought processes. The animator depicts his characters' emotions graphically in preference to imitating realistic human motion.

Snowdrift: John and Marsha can be viewed on YouTube.

Within you, without you: Analysing the character

'I had no idea of the character. But the moment I was dressed, the clothes and the makeup made me feel the person he was. I began to know him, and by the time I walked onto the stage he was fully born.... A tramp, a gentleman, a poet, a dreamer, a lonely fellow, always hopeful of romance and adventure.'

– Charlie Chaplin describing the creation of the 'Little Tramp' in *My Autobiography* (1964)

Using and avoiding typecasting in animation

The exercises in Chapter 1 gave us an opportunity to create something from nothing. The simple stick-figure, 'Sam', started to develop a character when his body attitudes were used to depict a variety of emotions. His personality developed further when he was given a prop to work with – or against. A simple ball could be used to express the character's inner emotions. Alternatively, it could become an adversary or a friend; an active or passive participant in the scene.

A distinctive costume or accessory makes a character easy to identify and tells us something about its personality before a move has been made or a word has been said. A tiger that wears horn-rimmed glasses like the cat in Chapter 1 (see page 15) can't be much of a threat. In the Snowdrift advert (see page 45), John's comb-over tells us that he is vain about his appearance despite advancing age. A towel wrapped around Goofy's head (see page 43) makes him look even less dignified than usual.

Animated characters are caricatures of reality, and designs for their homes, belongings and outfits are necessarily simpler than props and costumes for human actors. Animated characters can also have their personalities simplified, or over-simplified, so that they are clichéd 'types', rather than individuals – a handsome prince, a beautiful princess and so on.

Character 'types' should be the beginning and not the end of the animated performance. The animator's objective is to make the audience believe that a work of art is a living, thinking personality. Character *types* will behave *typically*. An *individual*, whether live or animated, will or will not do certain things in a given situation, based on its unique personality. A handsome prince with a personality based on one of your friends is far more interesting than a by-the-numbers 'type'.

It is important to remember that a character's personality can be based not only on what *is*, but what *may be*. Charlie Chaplin based his Little Tramp's character partially on his observations of poor people during his childhood in the slums of London, and partially on his hopes and aspirations. This contrast between artistic aspirations and poverty-stricken reality gives the Tramp a depth of character that keeps us watching Chaplin's films nearly a century after they were made.

Character performance, whether in animation or live action, cannot be based on theories in a book. The effectiveness of animated acting depends on the life experience of the animator and, more importantly, on their powers of observation. If you can empathise with a character, it doesn't even matter if you don't have a lot of life experience... you can animate a character that lives in France or on the moon without actually *going* there. As Jerome Stern writes:

'A broader application of *write what you know* recognises that the idea of *you* is complex in itself. You, in theory at least, know yourself. But your self is made up of many selves – the girl who wanted an older brother, the high school misfit, the college student who dressed in black and wanted to join the French club.... You are, in part, not only the person you once were, but also persons you have tried to be, persons you have tried to avoid being, and persons you fear you might be. All these are people you know.... Fiction based not on your own experience, but on experience you've observed is also writing about what you know. You know by empathy. You know by living.'

– © 1991 Jerome Stern, *Making Shapely Fiction*

I will add one more character to Mr Stern's excellent definition of '*you*' – in animation, you are also the person or character that you would *like to be*. In animation, you are not restricted by the limitations of the human body, or by constraints of time and space. Animation allows you to perform any character that you can *imagine*. You can be human, or animal, or both. There is absolutely no reason why a young animator cannot perform an old character or an older animator, a young one. All it takes is observation and a convincing depiction of a personality other than your own, as Art Babbitt discusses on the following page.

The sketchbook

Actors base their characters on their observation of other people. Animators observe people, animals, furniture – they take note of anything and everything, since an animator might be cast as an elderly person of the opposite sex or his/her cat or both characters simultaneously, with a tennis-playing dragon thrown in for good measure. Live-action reference for the last character might be a little hard to come by. The animator uses other methods.

It is essential for animators to keep sketchbooks so that their observations are preserved for later reference. It is not necessary to use a large sketchbook that can make people aware of the sketcher's presence (which can sometimes lead to awkward situations). Very small thumbnails can be drawn on slips of paper and pasted into the book later. These sketches can be used for animation inspiration years after the original drawings were made.

Ideally you should draw in your sketchbook for at least ten minutes every day. Don't just draw people sitting or standing still. Sketch figures in motion whenever possible. You will find that *no two people move in the same way*. Draw as many action sketches from life as you can, and keep them rough. Please do not draw from still photographs. A photograph will not give you the feeling of volume and movement that the living model will. You may sketch from DVDs of live-action films only if the DVD is never paused. (You may use slow-motion and repeat the clips.) Do not sketch from animated films since another artist has already analysed and caricatured the action.

> When I worked at UPA [the animation studio], despite the fact that the character of Mr Magoo had already appeared on the screen, I wrote a character study of Magoo that probably doesn't exist anymore. He had a richness that few people have taken advantage of. He knew that he was terribly nearsighted... he was practically blind. But he was trying to cover up his shortcomings with bluster, bravado. There were all sorts of opportunities there....
>
> You analyse a character not only for itself, physically and internally; you must analyse that character in relationship to the characters that surround him, the story as a whole, in relationship to his mood, and so on. As far as drawing is concerned, you of course always have to keep in mind the variance in movement among different characters.
>
> – Art Babbitt interview with Nancy Beiman (1979)

TIP

Recommended reading

The very best books on gesture drawing are the two volumes of *Drawn to Life: 20 Golden Years of Walt Disney Master Classes: The Walt Stanchfield Lectures*, by Walt Stanchfield and Don Hahn (Focal Press, 2009). Every animator or animation student will benefit from these incredible books.

2.4

Animal sketches

These drawings show the anatomy, characteristic poses, and movement of different animals. The dimensional quality of the drawings comes from observation of the actual animal; this quality is lost when two-dimensional photographs are copied or traced.

Animal sketches © 2008 by Adriana Pucciano

2.5

Action sketches

Quick action sketches are the artist's impression of fast movement rather than a literal depiction of reality.

Sketches © 2001 by Nancy Beiman

Quick sketches

The drawings of the tennis players (shown in Figure 2.5) took approximately five seconds apiece. Quick sketches will necessarily involve a certain amount of exaggeration or caricature, which is desirable for animation reference. Capture the impression of movement and don't worry about literally reproducing the model's appearance.

The action depicted in these sketches was very fast. Why not simply film a tennis match rather than sketch the players in real time? Live-action film of the tennis match can be very helpful. A motion picture lets you see the players in motion from different angles and study game moves in sequential order, but filmed action cannot substitute for personal observation and artistic interpretation.

Let us recall the Eadweard Muybridge photographic reference mentioned in this book's Preface (see page 9). If everyone uses the same filmed or photographic reference for their animated action, all animated tennis players/ horses and riders/actors will move in identical fashion. Your sketches from life reflect *your* view of the world and its creatures rather than a filmed and edited depiction of action frozen in time. Sketchbook drawings will provide you with a personal reference library that cannot be duplicated by another person and will keep your animation and character designs unique.

Sketches of real people in action can be used as reference for fantasy characters. That tennis-playing dragon mentioned earlier could use some of the poses captured in the human tennis sketches, suitably modified to account for its design, size, and ability to fly while using its wings and tail as a tennis racquet (see Figure 2.6).

Photography is also useful to the animator, particularly as reference for background and art direction. Photographic reference can be treacherous, however. A photograph eliminates the third dimension; this leads to the notorious 'flatness' of animation that is traced directly from individual frames of motion-picture film.

2.6

A dragon playing tennis

A flying dragon plays tennis using its wings and tail as a racquet. The earlier 'human' sketches were inspiration for the tennis poses and the flying sketches were based on drawings of cats, lizards, and birds.

© 2009 by Nancy Beiman

Get a mid-sized sketchbook or notebook with unlined pages. Draw some quick sketches in it every day, starting with your family, friends and pets (if available). These people and animals have characteristic gestures that will be familiar to you through repetition. Draw your subjects while they are moving, and work quickly (five to ten seconds per sketch for ten minutes per day.)

Feeling your way

Do not worry if the drawing 'doesn't look like' the subject. In animation, we say something **'feels'** right when we capture spirit and character through movement. If you can sketch quick action poses that **feel** right for that person, it might resemble him or her more than some formal portraits! Also sketch in public places – a playground, a tennis or basketball court, a beach, a farmer's market, or a picnic area – where you are **not** acquainted with the people. You may visit a gymnasium, cafeteria, or indoor market if the weather prohibits your working outdoors. Observe how no two human beings move in precisely the same fashion. See how different personalities are reflected in changing body attitudes and movements. Note the objects they own and the clothes they wear.

➤ Do you find people that you know easier to sketch than strangers?

➤ If you are in a market, what do the person's purchases say about them? How do different people carry their grocery bags?

➤ On a sports field, are some players more enthusiastic or aggressive than others?

➤ Can you convey a stranger's personality (as you see it) in your sketches?

➤ Do their clothing, body attitudes, and belongings indicate their personalities?

➤ Date all your sketches and write a brief description of the location as necessary.

➤ Keep all of your sketchbooks for future animation reference.

Note: If you are drawing in a playground you may want to ask permission from parents before sketching young children. Be unobtrusive while sketching in public.

Take a look at the reference footage. Then put it away and never look at it again.

– Frank Thomas, letter to Nancy Beiman (1985)

Next >

Next, we will analyse how to create a feeling of weight and volume in character animation.

Character volume, size and movement

'If size did matter, the dinosaurs would still be alive.'
– Wendelin Wiedeking, former CEO and President of the Porsche Automobile Company

The development of animated acting

Many early animated films featured graphic, highly stylised cartoon characters whose movement bore little resemblance to that of actual creatures. While 'rubber hose' characters can be amusing, it is difficult to create a subtle acting performance in this style of animation. Rubber-hose animation handles squash, stretch, and other distortions in a technique that calls attention to itself. Portions of a character's body might have its volume (the amount of space that the character's body displaces) violently distorted and deformed while other parts of the body remain motionless. Boneless arms may stretch and wave in the air like banners. A character's stomach might expand to an improbable size as it takes a deep breath and shrink down to normal volume again as it exhales. Large characters and small ones moved in identical fashion. As a result most character animation of the time does not create a convincing depiction of weight. The acting was as broad as the action, and action analysis was in its infancy.

2.7

'Rubber hose' animation
'Rubber hose' animation could distort portions of a character's body independently of the rest, giving the animation a 'weightless' quality.

As animators began to analyse living movement as a basis for caricatured action, more attention was paid to believable distortion of volumes in animation. The first change came in character design. Characters that were originally based exclusively on circular shapes were redesigned so that the arms and legs flowed 'organically' from a body that was influenced and shaped by the line of action. As discussed on page 29, the animators at the Disney studio used body attitudes rather than exaggerated mouth movements to animate believable dialogue scenes. These developments led to the use of more sophisticated animation and acting styles.

DVD reference: Character volume, size and movement

Snow White and the Seven Dwarfs (Walt Disney Studios, 1937) is a fantastic guide to differing movements of identically constructed characters. Watch the sequence where the Seven Dwarfs walk home from the mine singing the famous 'Heigh Ho' song – no two Dwarfs have the same body attitude during an identically timed walk, and Dopey even has a small skip added that shows how he is 'out of step' with the others.

Another great sequence to watch has the dwarfs kissing Snow White goodbye when they leave for work. Dopey and Grumpy show the strongest contrasts in movement and react *very* differently to Snow White's kiss! Bill Tytla's animation of Grumpy is a fantastic performance with great primary and secondary action, overlap and follow-through. Tytla animated each action in a different coloured pencil for better analysis.

Fantasia (Walt Disney studios, 1940) features the 'Dance of the Hours' sequence, with an elephant getting its foot caught in a very tenacious soap bubble, other elephants blowing through the air like leaves, an ostrich that floats above the crowd until gravity takes over and lands her on the stage with an audible thud, and an airily dancing hippo who squashes both her crocodile dance partner and the flimsy settee she sleeps on. Some of Preston Blair's marvellous animation is reproduced in his book *Cartoon Animation*.

Bully for Bugs (Warner Brothers, 1953) features a superbly animated bull that appears to weigh several tons. The animators create the feeling of the animal's immense mass using highly stylised and underplayed movements that contrast with the more frantic action on Bugs Bunny and a terrified matador.

Easy Street (Charlie Chaplin, 1917) Charlie Chaplin had a tremendous influence on early animators. This film is one of many that show how, and why, he is still an important influence today. The sequence where new policeman Charlie walks nervously beside a slum bully who matches his every step shows how the tremendous difference in body size and weight affects two identically timed walks. Chaplin attempts to stun the man with a blow from a stick in a great primary action that generates *no secondary action at all* on the bully. You may wish to compare Chaplin's performance with that of Bugs Bunny in *Bully for Bugs*.

We're all in this together

Animators found that an impression of solidity and weight could be created if *all* parts of the character's body were distorted during movement, though the distortion would not be equally strong in all areas. The movement of one part of the body would affect the whole. The forces of gravity, inertia, and muscle power would determine the degree (see Figure 2.8).

You can test this theory by extending one of your arms and waving it violently back and forth several times. If you are standing, your entire body will rock in opposition to each phase of the wave. If you are seated, your body will move less obviously, but the opposing action will affect the chair as well as your body. A violent movement on one side of the body will create a corresponding equal and opposing movement on the other side.

Newton's third law of motion states that 'For every action, there is an equal and opposite reaction.' Animation will vary from real life in this respect: while every action will generate an opposite reaction, it will not necessarily be an *equal* one. Unlike 'real life', an animated character's movement may emphasise or caricature the main action and underplay the opposing action for dramatic or comic effect. An animated character's actions and reactions may be impossible in real life, but believable in the animated context.

2.8

Distortion
A more believable sense of weight and volume is created when every part of the character's body is distorted during animated movement. Some parts will distort more than others, but every part of the character is affected by the forces of gravity, inertia, and muscle power.

Red arrows = waving arm. Ears rotate in opposite direction.

1	2	3	4	5	6	7	8
Belly moves from side to side in opposing action	Belly arcs up	High point of belly arc	Belly overlaps down as body heads up	Belly, arms, ears and cheeks overlap up as legs push off	High point of belly overlap	Feet extend to ground, stretching entire body as arms continue to arc up

2.9

Volume and weight
A violent action generates a corresponding and opposing secondary action on the rest of the character's body. Animated action is exaggerated, though not always this broadly, to create a feeling of volume and weight in drawn or rendered characters.

Note how the pig's violent arm movement in Figure 2.9 produces opposing action on the belly and ears. The belly first moves to the right in Pose 1 as the arm starts rotating left. The belly then rebounds to the left in Pose 2 and heads upward in Poses 3 and 4, rather like a bouncing ball, as the arm continues its arc. As the pig's arms complete their circular movement, the legs push the body up, and the weight in the belly drags downward in Pose 5 prior to recoiling up again during the leap in Pose 6 and 7, while the entire body reacts to the leg extension in Pose 8. The ears rotate in a complete circle as the pig's arm swings around its body. Each action is caricatured and the pig conveys a sense of volume and weight through its movement.

The organic distortion of all parts of an animated character during movement can be sketched in rough thumbnails. A CGI character must be specially rigged and each part carefully (and often separately) posed to create the asymmetrical distortion so effortlessly achieved by the drawings. CGI characters handled in a piecemeal fashion may appear weightless and the action will be unconvincing (see Poses a and b of Figure 2.10). New rigging techniques make it easier to translate the loose distortions of cartoon animation into modern CGI than was formerly the case, but the successful CGI animator must still be familiar with the effects of gravity, structural distortion, inertia, and outside forces on the entire character (Poses c and d).

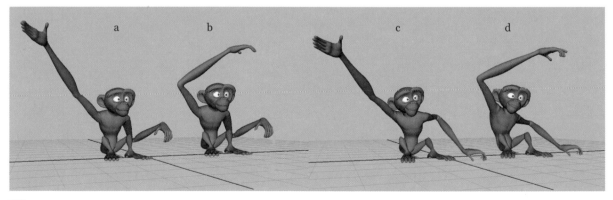

2.10

CGI

In Poses a and b, a CGI character moves its arm while the rest of the body remains perfectly motionless, creating stiff and unrealistic action. In Poses c and d, the arm movement affects the character's entire body.

Ape animation, design and rig © 2008 by Ignacio Barrios

Primary and secondary action: First things first

As stated earlier, not all parts of an animated character's body will be equally affected by movement. Some parts of the body will motivate the movement and other parts will be affected by this motivating force. Professional terms have developed to describe these forces:

- ✎ PRIMARY action
- ✎ SECONDARY action
- ✎ OVERLAPPING action and
- ✎ FOLLOW-THROUGH

Some confusion has arisen about what these terms actually mean. Here's an explanation.

Primary action is the main movement of the character. It can also cause a reaction on another character or object, or affect different parts of the same character.

Secondary action is influenced or created by a primary action.

Overlapping action involves drag and delay on different parts of a character's movement so that different parts move at different rates. This creates the impression of volume and weight in the movement.

Follow-through completes an action with a gradual slowing rather than a sudden stop.

The classic illustration of primary and secondary action has a character striking something. In Figure 2.11 the *primary* action is the swinging of the arm; the man's face reacts to the blow in *secondary* action. The girl's arm and hand move at different speeds; this is *overlapping* action. After the hit, the girl's arm and hair and the man's jowls *follow-through* instead of coming to an immediate stop. This adds weight and solidity to the action.

Primary and secondary actions will also affect different parts of one character's body, as you saw when you waved one of your extended arms back and forth. Your arm wave was the primary action; the opposing movement of your body was secondary action. In Figure 2.9 the illustrated pig waved its arms in a primary action, creating secondary action on its belly and ears.

To illustrate the concept of overlapping action, try standing up and turning around with every part of your body moving at the same rate. Your movements will resemble those of the Frankenstein monster (a brilliant acting performance by Boris Karloff, who was portraying the movements of an animated corpse). Animation that moves all at once is frequently mechanical-looking or lifeless (see Figure 2.12).

Primary action: arm anticipates up, moving in an arc. Secondary action on hair (violet).

a   b   c

2.11

Action and reaction
A *primary* action creates a *secondary* reaction with the *overlapping* action gradually diminishing in *follow-through*.

2.12

Frankenstein
Animated characters that move every part of the body at
the same time can appear stiff and lifeless.

Secondary action and follow-through on violet areas. Contact is implied, not shown, in 'e' (it makes the action stronger).

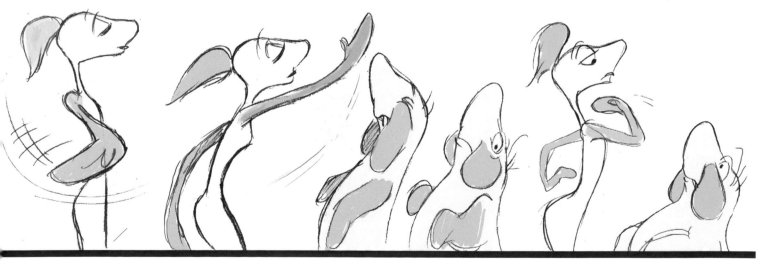

d   e   f

2.13

Simultaneous action

She jumps up and down and waves her arms in the air, all at the same time. Simultaneous action makes the animation appear stiff and artificial.

The grammar of animation

You can determine primary and secondary action by using a compound sentence to describe the scene before you begin thumbnailing or posing the character.

'**She jumps up and down** and *waves her arms in the air.*'

The primary action is described in the first part of the sentence. It is written in **bold** type and the secondary action is in *italics*. The primary action influences the secondary action. By moving different parts of the body at different rates, you create 'texture' in your timing.

The cheerleader in Figure 2.13 illustrates what can happen if you animate a character without considering primary, secondary and overlapping action. In this example, everything – body, hair, clothing, and props – has the same timing.

While this style of animation, like the rubber-hose style, can be amusing to watch, it is not the most effective way to convey complex acting performances or create a feeling of weight and volume in the character. And while some animators turn out beautiful work by going *straight-ahead* with a series of consecutive drawings or poses incorporating primary and secondary actions, the method isn't suitable for everyone. Here is an alternative way of performing the cheerleader's move.

Follow-through is a type of overlapping action where objects that cannot generate movement by themselves react to outside forces. The cheerleader's hair and skirt in Figure 2.15 are influenced by the movements of her body (the primary action), and the pompoms respond to the movement of her arms (secondary and overlapping action.) The hair and skirt are added last as follow-through.

These thumbnails are all for key and breakdown poses; they will be shot in pose test for timing. The inbetweens are never thumbnailed; they are added when the scene is being animated.

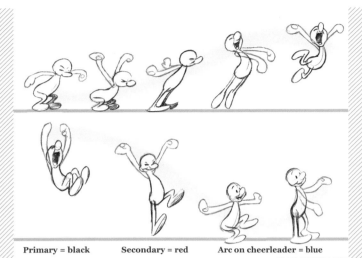

Primary = black   Secondary = red   Arc on cheerleader = blue

2.14

Primary and secondary action

The primary action ('*She jumps up and down*' – black drawing) is blocked in first. Secondary action ('*and waves her arms in the air*' – red drawings) is added afterwards. This adds *textured timing* to different parts of the character and gives it a feeling of weight and volume.

Pompoms overlap as line of action on arm reverses

Blue arrows indicate second reversal of line of action

Pompoms and arms reverse line of action a third time*

Arms continue arc reversal, with overlapping action on pompom

*Pompom arc follows body action here, but timing will differ

2.15

Overlap and follow-through

The cheerleader's pompoms *overlap* following the movement of her arms while her hair and skirt illustrate *follow-through*.

One, two, three: Animation priorities

I have always found it best to animate the primary, secondary, and overlapping action on the body first and leave the follow-through (clothing and hair) for last. When I was animating Billy Bones for *Treasure Planet* (Walt Disney Pictures, 2002) I first drew the lumbering body of the character and added his long, concealing cloak afterwards. The cloak draped over the underlying body shape and responded to Bones' movement. His walk was variably timed since he was injured. It was important to work out the asymmetrical movements of the walk first so that it would read even after most of the body was covered by the cloak (see Figure 2.17). When I tried to animate everything at once, I invariably found myself erasing and redrawing the cloak.

Practising the scales

Character *scale* (relative sizes) has a major influence on movement. Animated characters that work together are often designed with contrasting sizes and silhouettes. Think of Tom Cat and Jerry Mouse, the Roadrunner and Coyote, Bugs Bunny and Yosemite Sam, Shrek and Donkey, and Wallace and Gromit. Contrasting sizes make it easy to tell these characters apart. Contrasts are also created by the feeling of 'weight' in animation and by different lines of action, which make each character's movements unique.

Irving the Star-nosed Mole

and Ethel Worm

2.16

Irving the Star-nosed Mole and Ethel Worm
Contrasting sizes and shapes make it easy to tell
characters apart. They will also move differently due
to differences in perceived weight.

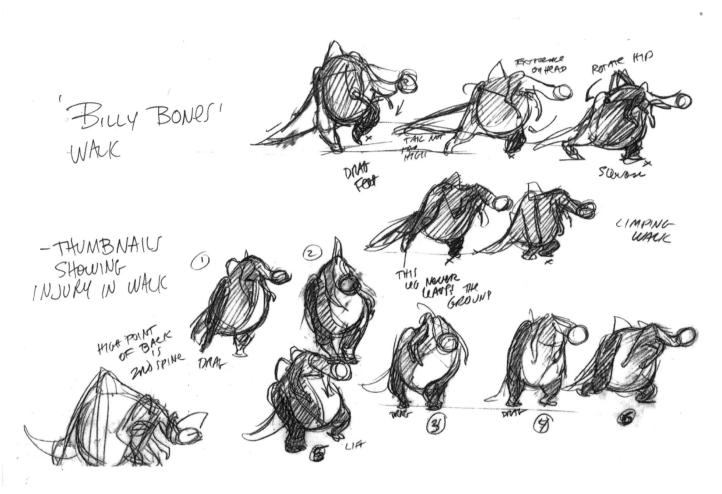

'BILLY BONES' WALK

-THUMBNAILS SHOWING INJURY IN WALK

DRAG FEET

TAIL NOT HIGH

EXTREME ON HEAD

ROTATE HIP

SQUASH

LIMPING WALK

THIS LEG NEVER LEAVES THE GROUND

HIGH POINT OF BACK IS 2ND SPINE

DRAG

LIFT

DRAG

DRAG

1 2 3 4 5

2.17

Asymmetry

Rough thumbnails for Billy Bones' walk showed the character body only. This is an asymmetrical walk for an injured character. Bones' long, concealing cloak was animated last so that it would properly *follow-through*.

Billy Bones © Disney Enterprises, Inc.

The same, only different

Other character teams such as the Dwarfs in *Snow White and the Seven Dwarfs* (Walt Disney Studios, 1937) actually shared the same basic construction, though their body volumes and lines of action varied. In instances such as these it is the body attitudes, timing and character acting that will develop distinct individuals from a standard design template. Identical human twins may have personalities that are wholly different; the same is true of animated twins.

Nobby and Bobby are identical twins. It is their birthday, and they both received the same toy as a present. Although their designs are exactly the same their reactions to the toy will be very different since we will assign different personalities to them. Nobby is a stubborn character who is *very possessive of his toys*. He is very pleased with the fine new present and doesn't want to share it with anyone else (see Figure 2.18).

Bobby, on the other hand, is very *bored* with this present and is going through the motions of playing with it. His attitude must be established before the action is thumbnailed (see Figure 2.19).

2.18

The stubborn twin
Nobby, the stubborn twin, loves his new toy and doesn't want to share. These thumbnails explore the action and acting for a scene where Nobby drops the ball and reacts by demanding it back. They will be shot as a pose test and adapted as keys for the final scene.

2.19

The bored twin
Bobby, the bored and spoiled twin, isn't very interested in playing with the new present and would rather be doing something else. These thumbnails show different attitudes that express his indifference. Some may be used for character model sketches rather than animation keys.

2.2 Identical characters with different personalities

Thumbnail and animate two short scenes where identical characters with different personalities interact with the same object. You may use Nobby and Bobby or use your own character designs – have them react to the ball or other inanimate objects. Animate each twin individually (we will have them working together in Chapter 7).

➤ First, write each twin's emotional characteristics on the top of the pages where you will draw your thumbnails. Use one page per character – do not draw them together at this time.

➤ Nobby's personality might be summarised as **'stubborn, selfish, likes the toy'**. What could develop from this sort of personality? Is he deliberately hiding this toy from his brother Bobby? You may add more descriptions that help you set his character. If you are using your own character, how can you best describe its personality?

➤ Bobby might be described as **'bored, spoiled and definitely uninterested in the toy'**. Think about his motivation. Is Bobby only keeping this toy so that his brother Nobby won't be able to play with it? If you use your own character, how does this twin's personality differ from that of the other?

➤ Next, thumbnail two short scenes showing each twin playing with the toy. Be sure to thumbnail each twin on a separate sheet of paper. If working digitally, save as separate files.

➤ Use a simple grid for the floor plane. Work rough – do not clean up your drawings.

➤ Each pose and action will be affected by their personalities. Be sure to keep them in character! Refer to your character descriptions when working.

➤ Shoot pose tests of the thumbnails of the keys and breakdowns in both scenes. Adjust the timing as necessary. Each scene should not be more than five or six seconds long. The action should be clear, simple and short.

➤ Use the same layout for both scenes. The characters should be the same size.

➤ Add timing charts, secondary and overlapping action as needed when inbetweening the animation for the final pencil tests.

➤ Shoot your final tests and edit them together.

➤ The identical twins have become two distinct personalities through their differing movements and their relationship with the toy.

He's not heavy... (not yet, anyway)

Different animated characters will ideally not all appear to be the same weight when moving. This is a major problem for the beginning animator. CGI animation makes it easy for the animator to maintain volumes and keep character appearances consistent (on model), but this advantage can turn into a disability if the rig doesn't distort sufficiently to convey the character's weight. Hand-drawn animation easily distorts, squashes and stretches, but can suffer from fluctuating volumes and go 'off model' very easily. Both types of animation can 'float' if the weight and size of the character do not affect its every movement. In animation, the term 'floating' refers to characters that appear weightless in a situation where movements and body masses should be affected by gravity or contact with solid objects. It is very common in CGI animation but can be avoided by using action analysis and textured timing. Floating is sometimes done deliberately, for example characters moving underwater will 'float' and convey solidity through drawing and perspective. The speed of their movements and reactions can indicate weight.

Weight and mass can be conveyed in two ways:

1. Distortion of the character or parts of its body.

2. Distortion of an object that the character comes into contact with.

A classic example comes in *Fantasia's* 'Dance of the Hours' sequence (Walt Disney Studios, 1940), which is a brilliant tour de force of action analysis where hippopotami and elephants are *simultaneously* weightless and massively heavy, and gravity is turned on and off like a light switch.

a

b

2.20

Distortion and overlap

Distortion and overlap of portions of the character's body help to convey a feeling of weight. Volumes of some body parts may distort differently from others. Distorting the entire body all the time can create a 'rubbery' feeling in the animation. Both techniques are appropriate depending on the circumstances of the scene and design of the characters. Heavy characters will also distort or deform objects that they come in contact with.

I always make a note of the character's weight, movement limitations (which may be present if the character is sick, old or injured) and personality, before starting to block out thumbnails for the animation. Some parts of the character's body may be harder or bonier than others. If you distort the entire body all at once all the time, the animation will appear 'rubbery', as if the character were gelatinous rather than solid. The 'bouncing ball' squashes will most strongly deform the sections that are contacting another surface or reacting to muscular force. This maintains the illusion of massive weight and a solid body. Of course this does not apply to all characters at all times, but it's a good guideline to follow.

Weight is conveyed by varying the timing of *overlapping action* on different parts of the body after the initial contact. For example, a lightweight mouse's whiskers, ears and tail will overlap after it leaps onto a piece of cheese, but its body will show more stretch than squash and its weight will have little effect on the cheese. A heavy elephant may have its gut overlapping after the initial squash when its foot contacts the ground, and its weight will strongly affect cheese, or any other surface that it contacts!

This is too fantastic even for animation – the elephant is weightless.

2.21

Floating
A 'floating' character does not deform when it contacts another surface; body parts maintain their integrity at all times instead of distorting during movement. The character appears to be weightless.

no inbetweens here!

'Real' elephants can't jump. Animated elephants have difficulty sitting in Chippendale chairs.

Next >

Next, let's talk about how sex affects a character's movement. (Do I have your attention?)

3

Is sex necessary?

Here we analyse differences in the animation of women and men – it's not just in the walk. A standard character design shows how sex may be communicated through acting without the use of secondary sexual characteristics. We return to the subject of dialogue animation and observe how male and female characters may actually use different mouth shapes when saying the same line of dialogue. The use and misuse of filmed reference is also discussed in the first section of this chapter.

The second part of the chapter discusses how the age and physical condition of an animated character will also influence its movements, and why not all animated characters necessarily 'act their age'.

Sex, age and attitude
The movement of these two characters differs by sex but is also affected by their age and their emotional attitudes.

Masculine and feminine character acting

'When dealing with people, remember you are not dealing with creatures of logic, but creatures of emotion.'

- Dale Carnegie, writer and lecturer

In 1979 I interviewed Art Babbitt, who was then working at the Richard Williams Studio. We spoke about animation and animated acting in particular. Babbitt answered my queries in such a gracious and humorous way that I've quoted him extensively in this chapter rather than paraphrasing our conversations. You can't improve on the words of a master:

'When you watch the back of a woman (which I still do at my age), you watch the swing of the skirt and the movement of her backside. You notice several things, and it varies with different women. The swing of a big, full, heavy skirt will have its extreme just a few frames after the swing of the buttocks. You'll also notice that in some cases the movement of the woman's backside is sort of *sharp*. It [the movement] is not smooth – it sort of whips from side to side – and I determined a long time ago that that's the kind of woman I don't want to have anything to do with.'

– Art Babbitt interview with Nancy Beiman (1979)

Men and women differ and *vive la différence!* – long live the difference! – as the French so aptly say. The obvious physical differences are the width of hips and shoulders, size of the breasts and skeletal shape. Men tend to have heavier frames with broader shoulders and greater upper-body strength than women. Women generally have broader hips with proportionately stronger legs and tend to be smaller than men. Of course generalities are just that. They do not apply in all cases, as we can see in the example of comedian Groucho Marx and comedienne Margaret Dumont.

3.1

Variations in size

The human frame will vary in size and build. Groucho Marx and
Margaret Dumont (seen here in *The Big Store*, 1941) demonstrate
that men are not *always* taller than women.

Yin and yang, together again

Early animated character designers would put a bow or ribbon on the head and a skirt around the waist of one basic character design largely composed of circles, and *voila!* The character design became female, as shown in Fig. 3.2. The female half of the animated 'team' was often posed with her weight borne on one leg so that her nonexistent 'hips' were emphasised. Male and female character movement would differ even at this early date. Minnie Mouse had a well-animated hip-swinging walk very early in her career (you can see a fine example of this walk in *The Delivery Boy* (1931) scene that was discussed in Chapter 1).

Betty Boop is the most famous female animated character from this period, or arguably from any American cartoon. She was the first animated female star not designed as the twin of a male character. This personification of the Jazz Age flapper was designed for the Max Fleischer Studio in 1929 by animator Grim Natwick, who gave Betty a mature woman's body and a (literal) baby face. The provocative combination of innocence and experience made her an instant sensation. Censors eventually insisted she tone down her saucy ways and cover her 'boop-boop-be-doop' with a high-necked concealing dress. Betty was reduced to playing second banana to an array of 'cute' or eccentric secondary characters and her audience appeal declined as a result. The story department at Fleischer's clearly did not know what to do with her. This change in Betty's fortunes need not have happened, since Betty (and her voice, Mae Questel) were good enough actresses to convincingly portray the downtrodden girl and lovely princess in Betty's only colour film, *Poor Cinderella* (1934). One wonders what might have happened had the Fleischer brothers asked Shamus Culhane, who worked for them after leaving Disney, to write a character analysis for Betty that allowed her personality to develop in the same way that Art Babbitt developed Goofy's. Betty Boop's charm and appeal keep her popular today even though she has not appeared in an animated film since her small but memorable cameo in 1988's *Who Framed Roger Rabbit*.

You will never win if you never begin

The early animators were nearly all male. Three of the early exceptions were Lillian Friedman Astor, who animated Betty Boop for the Fleischers, Retta Scott, who animated ferocious hunting dogs in Walt Disney's *Bambi* (1942), and Laverne (Verne) Harding who animated Woody Woodpecker at Walter Lantz's studio. Men have traditionally animated female characters and this practice has continued to the present day. There is no special reason for this. Animators of either sex can play male or female characters equally well. It is the acting ability of the animator that matters. Animation allows you to perform characters that you couldn't portray on stage (at least not if you want to be taken seriously). Animation eliminates any restrictions that age, appearance or sex might impose on your 'casting'. Joanna Quinn animates a devastating portrayal of male anatomy and egos in *Body Beautiful* (1991). Her hilarious and masterful caricatures are based on the meticulous observation of structure and movement in non-standard male and female body types (see Figure 3.3). The power of observation will give you the ability to create a personality other than your own through your animation.

> **Q:** When Jack Mercer [the voice of Popeye the Sailor] was in the armed services during World War II, you provided Popeye's voice for the cartoons as well as Olive Oyl's. How many films were done with you playing both characters?
>
> **Mae Questel:** [thinking] Let's see now, how many years was it? – Three!
>
> – Mae Questel, conversation with Nancy Beiman (1984). Vocal artists can be as versatile as animators. According to Jerry Beck, Mae Questel performed Popeye's voice in a number of Famous Studios cartoons released between 1945 and 1947. One example is *Shape Ahoy* (Famous Studios, 1945).

Impossible acts:
Combining reality and imagination

Some animators 'perform' a scene before beginning work on the drawings or poses. The drawbacks of this system are obvious. I once saw a male animator film his own walk before animating a walk on a young female character. The girl's walk became unmistakably masculine as a result of his relying too heavily on the reference material. He eventually got reference footage of a *woman* walking to use instead, but what did he do when he had to animate a scene with multiple characters? Did he film himself performing all of them separately and attempt to combine them when animating? If so, did all of the characters move the same way? Art Babbitt found that it wasn't possible to 'act out' some of the scenes he animated:

Q: I remember that in the Disney film *Moving Day* (1936), you animated a walk where Goofy's feet rotated backwards.

Art Babbitt: That's right. It's absolutely insane. If you studied the individual drawings, you just wouldn't believe it.

Q: Did you act the walk out before you drew it?

Art Babbitt: I *couldn't!* It was a physical impossibility. I do invented walks with characters now that just don't happen in real life. But on the screen, they're funny.

...It's all right if you use live action as a source of information. For example, I'm not a ballet dancer. I don't know all the steps. I don't know an *entrechat* from a *tour-en-l'air*, or whatever. So I think that it would be legitimate (if I was animating a ballet) to study a film of ballet to learn the steps.

But then, put away the live action – and I mean, put it ***away***. And then start to create. You ***animate your impression*** of what you saw. You **do not** animate a ***copy*** of what you have been looking at.

– Interview with Nancy Beiman (1979)

3.2

Willie and Billie Buzzard
A bow on the head, a skirt, and a pair of high heels were enough to differentiate boy from girl in the early days of animation.

3.3

Beryl and Vince
Beryl and Vince compete in the Body Beautiful competition.
Body Beautiful by Joanna Quinn © Beryl Productions

Walk on by

A walk is the most obvious way to show the difference between male and female character animation. A woman's skeleton has a wider pelvis, so her hips swing from side to side more noticeably than a man's when she walks. But there are other differences. Art Babbitt explained them to me:

Q: I feel that one of the reasons there has been a lot of rotoscope for the female characters is that guys don't move like women. They can animate a sexy girl walk, but the basic everyday way a woman moves is something that most guys can't act out for themselves. There is a difference.

Art Babbitt: Well, sure, there's a difference. But if they'd study how a woman moves, instead of some of her other attributes, they would know how to animate a woman moving. Just one little thing which is a caricature of life, and I'll have to show you what this is – it won't record on tape so you'll have to demonstrate it for your class – is this. It's a very simple thing. Generally, when we animate a man walking, his feet are parallel or almost parallel. Now you can take this simple walk of a man, and *by simply making the feet go in a straight line*, the walk becomes *feminine*. Now watch. (Swings one foot in front of the other as he walks.)

Q: Women do tend to swing their feet around in front like that?

Art Babbitt: I don't know that real women swing their feet around that way, but *in animation* you can make the walk *appear* feminine.

You can also make a man walk that way. You can make a man walk with his feet overlapping all the way. There are all sorts of possibilities. But the main thing I wanted to bring out was that just that one little change of taking the feet off the parallel, changes the walk from masculine to feminine.... There are feminine movements of the body in the hands, the head, the tilt of the head. I think the main reason male animators don't do too well with female characters, unless they use rotoscope as an aid, is simply because they've never *studied* enough....

– Interview with Nancy Beiman (1979)

Feet move on parallel lines

One foot swings in front along a single line

The same design may appear male or female

3.4a

The way you walk
A woman can walk with her feet in a straight line like a cat's while a man's feet can move on parallel lines. Generic characters will appear to be male or female if the foot placement and hip movements vary.

1 2 3 4 5 6 7 8 9 10 11 12

3.4b

The runway walk
The 'runway walk' exaggerates the foot and hip swing.
Animation and design from *Cartoonal Knowledge*
© 2008 by Doug Compton

1 2 3 4

3.4c

A masculine walk
An exaggerated 'masculine' walk shifts the body weight over the contact foot with strong shoulder action.

The royal walk

The 'royal walk' that Art Babbitt refers to in the quote below resembles a 'feminine' walk along a straight line minus the swing of the hips, while the 'devious' walk he created is invented action. It is believable rather than realistic, with side-to-side movements that indicate the character's mental state as well as his status. Every animated performance depends on a combination of the animator's skill, the story point, the character's design and function in the story, and the film's soundtrack.

You can see how important sound is to animation if you view a film's climax (for example Monstro the Whale chasing Geppetto and Pinocchio at the end of *Pinocchio*) with the volume control set at zero. The action, while still exciting, appears slower without the soundtrack's support.

We are at a disadvantage here since this book contains no soundtrack. So let's get one.

Mood music sets the relationship

Animators are sometimes described as 'actors with pencils' – or styli, or tablets, or puppets, depending on your medium. I have always felt that animation resembles *dance* more than stage or screen acting. Animation, like dance, uses choreography, varied rhythms, and motion arcs. Both create performance through stylised movement – dialogue, or song, is secondary action. I usually animate while listening to music that fits the mood and rhythm of the scene.

You do not need to be a dancer to animate effective dance scenes any more than you need to be an elephant to animate one successfully. Analyse the rhythm of the music and view films of dancers, if necessary. Then *put your film reference away* and thumbnail dance steps, real or invented, the same way you would for any other scene. If you work to the rhythm, even invented actions will read as dance. The dance of the mind translates to a graceful performance on the screen.

> Now a **royal** walk would be straight ahead, like at a wedding or a funeral. But in this case [the character] slips from side to side. His walk is as devious as he is.... I don't know whether the audience will get the subtlety of this being related to his deviousness or not; that is unimportant. The fact is that a character is being created that is unlike those that we normally see. **You can invent action in animation.**
>
> – Art Babbitt interview with Nancy Beiman (1979)

3.5

A royal walk
A 'royal walk' incorporates some feminine movement – the
feet swing in front of one another along a straight line, but hip
movement is downplayed, producing a 'gliding' effect.

3.1 Male and female walks

Animate two walks, one with a male and one with a female version of Sam, or another generic character, timed to instrumental music that helps set the emotional mood.

➤ Locate one or two short pieces of instrumental music that will help you portray the mood of a male and a female character in an animated walk cycle.

➤ You may use different pieces of music for the two tests, or you might animate the male and female characters to the same musical track using the same emotional state for both. (This is the harder assignment!)

➤ Do not feel obligated to use sweet, light classics for a female character, or heroic themes for a male. You may use any music that suggests a personality or attitude to you as long as there are no lyrics. (Lyrics distract from the action.)

➤ You may wish to write the attitude that you want the characters to express on a piece of paper before searching for the music.

➤ Write the attitude and the title of the musical track on each scene's thumbnail page.

➤ Some sample musical themes and suggested emotions are listed here. There are of course many other possibilities – use whatever appeals to you.

Dramatic: Triumphal march from 'Aïda' by Giuseppe Verdi

Sad: 'Funeral March' by Frédéric Chopin

Joy: Wedding March from 'A Midsummer Night's Dream' by Felix Mendelssohn

Ominous or devious: 'In the Hall of the Mountain King' by Edvard Grieg

Delicate: 'The Dance of the Sugarplum Fairy' by Peter Tchaikovsky

Cool: 'Happy-Go-Lucky Local (Night Train)' by the Oscar Peterson Trio

Comic: 'An American in Paris' by George Gershwin

Frantic: 'Sabre Dance' by Aram Khachaturian

➤ Thumbnail the two scenes while listening to the music. Let your acting portray the character's sex and attitude. Do not draw hair, clothing, or secondary sexual characteristics.

➤ Now animate two walk cycles, female and male, in your chosen emotional attitudes, using the musical beats as a timing guide. Use a simple prop if you need to.

➤ Shoot a pencil test of your thumbnails. You may wish to synchronise the music with the final test, although it should work well without it.

➤ Show the finished animation tests to an audience. Can the viewers determine the character's sex and attitude from its movements?

Double bounce walk cycle

to *La Belle Excentrique* (Satie)

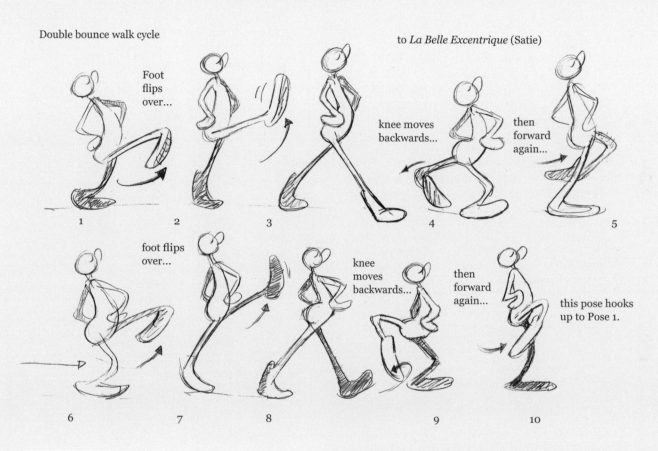

Foot
flips
over...

knee moves
backwards...

then
forward
again...

1   2   3   4   5

foot flips
over...

knee
moves
backwards...

then
forward
again...

this pose hooks
up to Pose 1.

6   7   8   9   10

3.6

A feminine walk

La Belle Excentrique by Eric Satie provided inspiration for
a feminine walk with 'invented action' – believable, but not
realistic.

Getting in touch with your inner woman or man

The female character's walk is not the only point where she differs from the males. All of a female character's animation will be handled differently, including dialogue.

Figure 3.7 shows a performance of the line 'I told you not to do that' by Sam, the generic character from Chapter 1. Sam's design shows no secondary sexual characteristics, so we are going to let the key poses show us whether Sam is male or female. Here, the tilt of the head and action on the hands adds to the 'feminine' feeling. The 'male' character gestures tend to be more direct even when the character is making a subdued point. Animated action can suggest sexual differences on identical character designs without the trappings of clothing, hair and make-up.

Figures 3.8 and 3.9 show thumbnails of a male and female character shouting the same line of dialogue. The drawings portray exaggerated mouth shapes, but even the grossest distortions will be less extreme on the female character because of her 'lighter', more feminine design.

I   **told you not**   **to do that**

3.7

Body language
A feminine or masculine reading of a line is determined by the body language, position of the head and hands, and differences in facial expression. A basic design can perform as either a male or female character.

3.8

Male dialogue
'I told you not to do that!' Dialogue mouth shapes will vary depending on the voice track and the mood as well as the character design. Phonetic dialogue is written under each key pose.

I told you   *not to*   *do that*

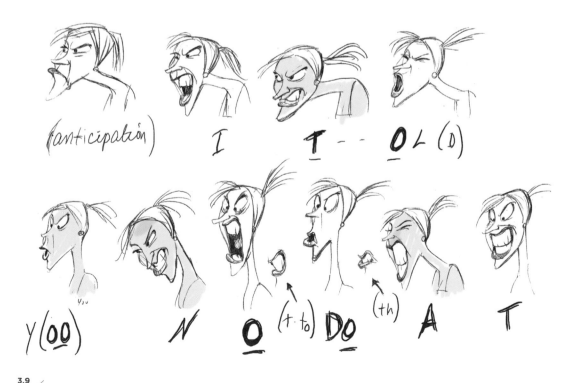

(anticipation)   I   T - - O L (D)

Y (OO)   N   O   (t.to) DO   (th) A   T

3.9

Female dialogue

Female lip synch, even when exaggerated, is generally less extreme than that of a male character. The drawings in red are breakdown poses between two extremes. Some lines are 'cheated' – for example, the word 'that' is pronounced through clenched teeth.

3.2 Male and female dialogue

➤ Animate two scenes of Sam or another generic character using the same line of dialogue. Have it use feminine acting in the first test, and be masculine in the second.

➤ Stage the character from the waist up so that its arms are in the scene. You can find dialogue online or record it yourself.

➤ **The sex of the actor reading the line is not important.** Your animation will portray the sex of the character.

➤ Keep the scene short (not more than five seconds).

➤ Determine where Sam is looking (the **eyeline**) before starting the scene. Is Sam talking to someone or something offscreen? Is he/she talking to us? Keep the eyeline consistent when animating.

➤ Write the sex and emotional state of the character at the top of the page that you draw your thumbnails on. Explore different ways of portraying the emotion and use the poses that work best for you as guides for the animation keys.

➤ For reference, use your sketchbook drawings of women and men in motion. You may wish to sketch additional reference material for facial expression before beginning the exercise.

➤ You may use a prop if desired, or combine this exercise with Exercise 3.3.

➤ Scan your thumbnails and shoot a pose test to time the key poses; then animate your scenes and synchronise the dialogue to the finished tests.

➤ Show the finished animation tests to an audience. Can the viewers determine which character is male and which is female from its movements?

Next, we will show Sam interacting with a simple prop while performing as male and female characters. Femininity is usually associated with noticeably curving, smooth arcs in animated movement; a masculine quality might be achieved with more direct movement and less pronounced arcs. The tilt of the head and additional overlap on an arm during movement might also suggest femininity. Masculine and feminine animated movements may also differ in intensity. There is no 'absolute' standard; circumstances will alter cases.

➤ Animate two brief scenes (not more than five seconds apiece) one with a male and one with a female version of Sam, or another generic character, interacting with a simple prop.

➤ Use a simple bouquet of flowers. Stage the action from the waist up.

➤ Consider the emotional state of the characters when planning your scenes. Each character may react happily or lovingly after receiving a gift, but other variations are possible.

– Is the character receiving flowers from someone whom he or she does not love?

– Is a gift of flowers being returned by someone who does not love him or her?

– Is someone allergic to flowers?

➤ Concentrate on clarity of poses and the quality of the acting. **You may be transitioning between two emotions in this exercise.** A sad character may be cheered by the flowers, or vice versa. Make sure that both emotions read well.

➤ Write the sex and emotional state(s) of the character at the top of each scene's thumbnail page. This will keep your thoughts focused on the purpose of the scene. Write the timing for any emotional changes; are they **gradual** or **sudden**?

➤ First thumbnail or pose the movements of the body, using a simple triangular shape for the bouquet. Individual flowers may be added if they are important to the scene, but don't add a lot of unnecessary detail.

➤ **Try combining this exercise with Exercise 3.2 (Male and female dialogue).** How does your choice of dialogue influence or change the pantomime acting?

Unusual behaviour

In order to animate movement that is not normal for your character (perhaps 'drunk' or 'injured' comes to mind) it is essential that you first know how it *normally* moves. For example, a walk throws the human body off-balance. A drunken man or woman has lost this sense of balance yet, for comedy's sake, never quite falls. The best way I found to handle this type of action was to animate the head and upper body first in a weaving action, then add the legs moving forward or backward as necessary to get under the centre of gravity and catch the weaving body just before it falls. The arms are added last as secondary action. The legs can attempt to form some of the poses that you used during the normal walk or run (see Figure 3.11). You may find that straight-ahead animation also gives you the effect you want. It is easier to caricature animated movement after you have analysed the character's skeletal construction, weight and balance.

3.10

Moving mammoths
Living animals can provide reference for extinct species with similar skeletal construction. In this scene from *Ice Age: The Meltdown* (2006), Manny the Mammoth's animation is based on an elephant. Ellie believes that she is an opossum and attempts to move like one. Action analysis of extinct animals is discussed in Chapter 5 (see page 130).

Courtesy of 20th Century Fox/The Kobal Collection

HEAD, BODY + LEGS THUMBNAILED FIRST...

ROTATE LEG
ROTATE HEAD

CHEAT THE ARM- IT STAYS IN FRONT OF BODY

CHEAT ARMS! THEY DO NOT ROTATE!

DRUNK WALK- REALLY OFF-BALANCE ATTEMPT AT A CONFIDENT WALK.

3.11

Drunken walk
A drunken walk is most successful when you first analyse how the character moves when it is *not* drunk.

Next >

We have seen how character animation can portray basic sexual differences in generic characters; in the next section we will consider how the *age* of the character influences its thought processes and acting.

The ages of man (and woman)

Gait (n.) a person's manner of walking.

The riddle of the Sphinx

We have seen how animation can portray female and male characters without relying on secondary action (such as hair or clothing) or obvious differences in character design. Now it's time to investigate the differences in movement between young, adult and elderly human characters. The character's age will be just as influential as its sex if not more so.

Human locomotion is neatly described in the famous riddle that the Sphinx asks travellers en route to Thebes:

'What goes on four legs in the morning, on two legs at noon, and on three legs in the evening?'

Oedipus answers the question correctly: 'A man, who crawls on all fours as a baby, walks on two legs as an adult, and walks with a cane in old age.'

The Sphinx 'destroyed herself' after Oedipus passed his test. Don't worry; the tests in this chapter will have non-fatal outcomes, though the lessons will be just as important.

Expressing age through movement: The beginning

Human beings (along with insects, frogs and other amphibians) are creatures that move in completely different ways during our different stages of development. This interesting situation is due partly to human beings' lengthy childhoods and partly due to the design of our bipedal skeletons. We are a member of the very small fraternity of Earth creatures that have ever walked on two legs. There is no question that bipedal locomotion is not the easiest way of getting around. Four-legged walkers are like tables with the weight evenly divided over the four 'corners'. Walking on two legs is more like balancing on stilts. A bipedal walk is a series of falls and recoveries; you balance on one stilt and swing the other stilt forward to shift your weight and your balance to it before you fall on your face, then repeat as needed. (A drunk lacks a sense of balance, which is why drunken stumbling walks, near-falls and recoveries are so much harder to animate than a normal walk.) And what a variety of gaits humans use to get around! We walk, tiptoe, trot, run, jump, hop, skip, strut, shuffle, stumble, and (when the mood takes us) perform movements in rhythm that are called *dance*.

3.12
Don't walk/walk: The effects of age
The Sphinx's riddle describes how age affects human locomotion.

3.13
Bipedal gaits
Bipedal gaits are more varied than those of quadrupeds; as with
most human actions, there is no absolute standard.

A leg at each corner

An infant human's head is proportionately enormous, measuring approximately one-third of the total body length. Infant legs are bowed and extremely short in relation to the torso. A baby's legs are not strong enough to support its weight while standing until the child is nearly one year old.

So the riddle of the Sphinx is literally true. We do have more 'legs' when we are small since an infant human crawls on all fours. The movement pattern of the child's legs is nearly identical to the walk of a four-legged animal but not as efficiently done. Crawling babies move with their arms and legs on the diagonal – right front/left rear, left front/right rear as in Poses b and c of Figure 3.14. The child carries the weight on hands and knees rather than on the toes as the cat in Pose d is doing. There are no standard movements. The child in Pose a is using a straight-legged quadruped walk. An infant has just taken possession of its body and isn't familiar with the operating instructions.

Here are some observations on infant human movement. See how many other characteristics you can add after observing an infant from life.

- Movements are asymmetrical and inconsistently timed; the legs and arms are not always under control.

- Frequent falls onto tummy or backside, sometimes with crying, sometimes with no change in reaction (and usually no injury).

- Crawl will resemble four-legged animal walk 'on the diagonal'.

- Movements might appear aimless; a waving arm might precede a leg movement, and an action might originate at either the top or the bottom end.

3.14

Infant locomotion

Infant locomotion is more enthusiastic than efficient, and it is never consistent. Crawls will resemble a quadruped's 'walk on the diagonal'.

Baby steps

A child between the ages of one and two years who is learning to walk is called a 'toddler'. Toddler heads are still very large in relation to their bodies, giving them a very high centre of gravity located in the chest area rather than near the belly button like that of an adult human. This (and nappies or diapers) give toddlers a precarious sense of balance and a characteristic waddling walk.

Interestingly enough, many animated characters have 'infantile' or toddler proportions and features that are designed to appeal to our sense of 'cuteness'. Lilo, the heroine of *Lilo & Stitch* (Walt Disney Pictures, 2002), is a seven-year-old girl who was deliberately designed with the body of a two-year-old child. Lilo is nearly three 'heads' high – the same proportions as Mickey Mouse. Stitch the alien is approximately two 'heads' high; he would have been terrifying, not cute, with a more adult body. Both characters were animated with purposeful, adult movements despite their babyish proportions.

Animated children may be adults in diapers. 'Baby' Herman was a grown man trapped in an infant body in *Who Framed Roger Rabbit* (1988). Midget criminal 'Baby Face Finster' found an infantile disguise useful when robbing banks and fooling Bugs Bunny in *Baby Buggy Bunny* (1954). Five-year-old starlet Darla Dimple was the villain of *Cats Don't Dance* (1997). Contrasting a character's acting and action with its appearance is a great acting challenge for an animator.

3.15

Toddler locomotion
Toddlers' short legs and high centre of gravity result in a waddling walk with frequent falls but infrequent injury, since they're not too far off the ground.

Baby Herman: For crying out loud, Roger, I don't know how many times we have to do this damn scene! Raoul, I'll be in my trailer, taking a nap!

[Walks between a woman's legs]

Baby Herman: 'Scuse me, toots.

– Who Framed Roger Rabbit (1988)

DVD reference: Acting your age

Lilo & Stitch (Walt Disney Pictures, 2002): Lilo is a seven-year-old girl designed with a two-year-old toddler's body. Stitch has even more infantile proportions. Both move with the agility of preteens. Lilo's sister Nani has an adult woman's body and movement but thinks like a teenager.

The Triplets of Belleville (Les Armateurs, 2003): We first meet the title characters as young women designed and animated in the 'rubber hose' style. We next see them 30 years later as extremely active 'little old ladies' animated in a caricatured-realism style. Director Sylvain Chomet had his animators study the movements of elderly women and youthful basketball players to give the triplets the right mixture of age and agility.

Robin Hood (Walt Disney Productions, 1973): Prince John is a wonderful combination of infant and adolescent. The false king sucks his thumb, whines, and throws temper tantrums.

Baby Buggy Bunny (Warner Brothers, 1954): Chuck Jones based midget bank robber 'Baby Face Finster' on a character from Todd Browning's early talkie *The Unholy Three* (1925). Watch Finster's proportions change from 'baby' to 'adult' as his outfits change.

Who Framed Roger Rabbit (Robert Zemeckis, 1988): Maroon Cartoons star 'Baby' Herman performs as an infant but offscreen he is a middle-aged, cigar-smoking lecher trapped in an infant's body.

Cats Don't Dance (Turner Feature Animation, 1997): Darla Dimple is the film's five-year-old villainess. In the 'Big and Loud' song sequence this 'cute' little girl performs showgirl-style bumps and grinds and displays the jealous personality of a spurned, 'adult' diva.

Some Like It Hot (Billy Wilder, 1959): Marilyn Monroe gives one of her funniest and best performances as 'Sugar' Kane, the adult singer with a childlike personality. The film is also notable for Tony Curtis and Jack Lemmon's more-or-less successful adoption of female personae and for one of the most famous closing lines in motion-picture history.

Brats (Hal Roach Studio, 1930): Laurel and Hardy are hilarious as children being babysat by fathers who are as immature as they are. The comedians beautifully combine their typical movements with those of six-year-olds.

Acting the (infantile) part

Live actors have personified the contrast between infantile behaviour and adult appearance. Comedians Laurel and Hardy played fathers and (identical) sons in *Brats* (1930). Stan Laurel's childlike 'cry' became one of his most famous routines (see Figure 3.16).

Animated films also portray this contrast. Prince John in *Robin Hood* (Walt Disney Productions, 1973) sucks his thumb and pulls his ear when stressed and throws temper tantrums when he does not get his way. Though nominally an adult and a King, Prince John's personality combines infantile self-centredness and adolescent stubbornness. His scraggly mane even resembles an adolescent's first attempts at a beard. Peter Ustinov gave the Prince a whiny, snivelling voice that inspired Ollie Johnston's bravura animation. Infancy can be in the mind as well as in the body.

Certain attitudes and actions will create the impression of immaturity in an animated character's performance, whether or not they are designed with infantile proportions. Here are some characteristics of the infant human mind:

- ✎ Curiosity; everything is new and all things are equally interesting.
- ✎ Short attention span; easily distracted.
- ✎ Slow reaction time; screaming does not immediately start after a fall; the infant takes a few seconds to adjust to the new situation.
- ✎ Emotions are expressed openly.
- ✎ Trusting attitude; acceptance of everything around them.
- ✎ Body image is not set; portions of body may be treated as props.
- ✎ Self-centred; does not consider other points of view.
- ✎ Possessive. (It's *mine!*)

(Can you think of any others? How many of these immature thought patterns might also appear in adult characters?)

Animate Sam, the test figure from Chapter 1, performing as an 'infant'.

➤ Thumbnail a short scene (five to seven seconds long) in which Sam acts as if he/she were an infant.

➤ Do not change the adult proportions of the character.

➤ Some suggestions for the action might be:

(a) Sam tries to walk, then falls down and begins to cry after realising he fell (infantile reaction).

(b) Sam loses a toy and reacts by throwing a tantrum.

(c) Sam discovers a new toy and is fascinated with it. (The 'toy' could be his or her foot, or you may use a simple prop.)

➤ Thumbnail as many 'infantile' poses around these ideas as you can think of. Then shoot a pose test of the drawings and time the action.

➤ This pose test may be different from your earlier ones since infantile action is often unfocused and an infant's attention span is short. Try shooting your thumbnails more than once in different order, changing the timing as necessary, to see if this gives your acting a more infantile quality.

3.16

Infantile adult characters
Adult characters may exhibit infantile behaviour. Stan Laurel and Oliver Hardy played both themselves and their children in *Brats* (Hal Roach Studios, 1930).
Courtesy of Hal Roach/MGM/The Kobal Collection

Kidding around

School-age boys and girls are often as agile as young cats. They can perform violent actions that can and do give their parents the vapours. This is because they are still small and light enough to avoid injury – most of the time.

Differences between boys' and girls' movements, and anatomy, become much more obvious when they reach puberty. Teenagers are growing so fast they must get re-acquainted with their rapidly changing bodies. As our mothers told us, 'It's just a stage you're going through.' And what a 'stage' it is. Legs and necks and arms grow at different rates in the adolescent body, sometimes making teenagers' movements appear awkward. Teenagers may also display rapid changes in emotions as a result of their physical changes. An adolescent personality can be conveyed by having the character's mood change within the scene. Take care not to change emotions too quickly; each one must be held long enough so that we understand the character's thought processes. Try animating a scene with a character that is a caricature of yourself as a teenager (if you dare!)

This 'leads' us to an interesting way of showing the different 'Ages of Man' by varying which part of the body moves first.

3.17
Children
Young boys and girls are both extremely active.

> “
> ...Then, the whining schoolboy with
>   his satchel
> And shining morning face, creeping
>   like snail
> Unwillingly to school.
>
> – William Shakespeare, *As You Like It* (Act II, Scene VII)
> ”

3.18
Teenagers
Teenagers are sometimes self-conscious and easily embarrassed by their changing bodies. An adolescent character may also have a highly changeable disposition. Moods are intense and strongly felt and more than one emotion may be present in a scene.

Expressing age through movement II or: Leading with your left

Once upon a time in England, I attended a lecture given by a very good actor whose name I have forgotten. The young man explained that young, old, or middle-aged characters could be portrayed by one actor by simply varying the part of the body that *'leads'* movement. (The *lead* is defined as the first part of the body to move. Professional fighters and golfers will *'lead'* with either the right or the left arm when striking an opponent or ball. Dancers *'lead'* with the right or left foot and can *change leads* during the dance.)

The young actor proceeded to demonstrate how changing a lead on a human walk could indicate a character's age. He first demonstrated 'a young lover' by making flowery movements with his arms, throwing out his chest, and moving in great leaps that made him appear to float above the ground. In the middle of one leap, he 'tripped' over an invisible rock. The lover acknowledged the rock momentarily without changing his blissful attitude, then proceeded onward, his movements as high as his spirits.

...And then the lover,
Sighing like furnace, with a woeful ballad
Made to his mistress' eyebrow...

– William Shakespeare, *As You Like It* (Act II, Scene VII)

Takes one step after tripping...   (hold)   ballet move on legs... joyous reaction...   continue leaping as before.

3.19

A man in love
All the world loves a lover, and this one loves even the rock that trips him up.

Maturity and age

The actor then showed how a very confident mature man might move by 'leading' with his chin or his chest. It was amazing to see how the movements of his entire body were affected by changing the lead. In animation parlance, the *line of action* became completely different and a new character was created with each change. Interestingly enough, quick movements with a 'lead' on the chin appeared arrogant, but slower timing with the same lead could indicate a more cautious character. (And a *woman* who leads with her chest creates still *another* type of character!)

Finally, the actor showed how an extremely aged man might walk. He led *all* his movements with his knees! He was forced to lower his centre of gravity and take slow, hobbling steps.

A single actor was able to play characters of different ages without changing his costume or applying make-up. He accomplished this by varying his 'lead' – but only portrayed *male* characters. Do women 'lead' differently? Well, sometimes they do, as Art Babbitt pointed out to me:

Art Babbitt: ...Just this morning, I saw a woman walking. [She] was a refutation of the general concept of how a woman moves.... You always think of a prize fighter as swinging from side to side. Well, here was a case where a woman was walking that way. In fact, I encounter her every morning when she walks her dogs up a hill.

Q: Was she very heavy?

Art Babbitt: Fairly heavy, yeah. And she walked [shifting the weight] from side to side.

Q: I've seen how very fat women or pregnant women will walk like a man, because they haven't got the movement in the hips.

Art Babbitt: Well, you'll also notice how other things [in a woman's walk] are affected by something that has happened to her. A pregnant woman will often walk leaning *slightly backwards*. She's trying to balance the weight of the baby in her stomach. That's also called 'mother's pride'. I got that out of a book on nursing before I determined on my career.

–Art Babbitt interview with Nancy Beiman (1979)

Remember to consider your character's past memories, present age, and physical condition when animating a scene. Technical skill is very important in animation, but it is your power of observation, acting ability, sense of caricature, and imagination that will *lead* you to create memorable character performances.

> Then a soldier,
> Full of strange oaths, and bearded like the pard,
> Jealous in honour, sudden, and quick in quarrel,
> Seeking the bubble reputation
> Even in the cannon's mouth...
>
> The sixth age shifts
> Into the lean and slipper'd pantaloon,
> With spectacles on nose, and pouch on side,
> His youthful hose well sav'd, a world too wide,
> For his shrunk shank...
>
> – William Shakespeare, *As You Like It* (Act II, Scene VII)

3.20

Leading with the chin or chest
Leading with the chin or chest could signify military bearing or combativeness in general. Slowing down the timing can make the same *lead* appear timid or cautious. A female character creates a completely different impression.

3.21

Leading with the belly
Leading with the belly can indicate a middle-aged character.

3.22

Leading with the knees
Leading with the knees limits the actor's body movements, mimicking the frailties of old age.

3.23

Overweight and pregnant women
A stocky or overweight woman might walk a bit like a man, with less movement in the hips than normal. A pregnant woman will walk leaning slightly backward to balance the weight over her body's centre of gravity.

At my age, I get up in the morning, go into the bathroom and look in the mirror to see what FELL OFF during the night!

– Frank Thomas (age 88, in conversation with Nancy Beiman)

Next >

We will next consider animal characters and the people they resemble.

4

Animal actors

In this chapter the action and acting of birds and beasts is analysed and compared to that of human actors. You will learn the principle of 'animation by association' where the action of different species and substances are blended in animation to convey the 'feel' of an animal's movements rather than a literal representation of reality. A human/bird caricature and a winged horse are analysed in an interview with animator Ellen Woodbury in the second section.

Human acting becomes richer when associated with animal characteristics, and the third section of this chapter provides some examples. Finally, you will learn how simple crawling creatures can reduce animation to its absolute minimum – the line of action.

Varied expressions
An animated dog can use human or animal expressions
or even both simultaneously.

Four legs good, two legs better? Creating animal characters

'[Lady and Tramp eating spaghetti] were based on me and my wife [Jeanette]. Not on how we looked, but how we **felt** about each other.'
– 'Frank Thomas, conversation with Nancy Beiman

Skeletal comparison and action analysis

Animated animals are often people in fur suits. They may move like quadrupeds, but their sentiments, emotions and desires are human. This familiar behaviour helps us identify with their problems so that we relate to other species on our own emotional level.

Animal anatomy and animal drawing books should be an important part of your library. (Some suggested titles are listed in the 'Inspiration and Reference' section at the end of the book.) You will find that quadruped and human anatomy have many similarities. A paw or hoof is a modified 'hand' and you can easily recognise knees, heels, upper and lower arms, and other corresponding bony structures in animal and human skeletons. Proportions of the bones will vary, but the vertebrate skeleton is a variation on one basic theme.

A quadruped, like a table, has 'a leg at each corner' with the body weight balanced over all four feet. The centre of gravity may vary slightly by species but is generally located in the rib cage just behind the shoulder blade. The pelvis and spinal column show the greatest difference between biped and quadruped. A human pelvis is basket-shaped and the spinal column has an S-curve which makes it easier to balance the body for an upright stance. A quadruped's spine is curved like the letter C and the pelvis is flat. This, along with a high centre of gravity, makes it hard for the quadruped to support the body on its hind legs.

Even our close relatives the apes have a spine and pelvis designed for walking on all fours, which is why they are not able to stand or walk fully upright for very long. Conversely, human beings find it difficult to walk on all fours since human legs are proportionately far longer than our arms. As we saw in Chapter 3, a crawling human can duplicate the movement of a quadruped by travelling on hands and knees.

Quadruped animals have 'standard gaits' (methods of moving) that can be analysed and caricatured in animated performance. They are:

1. The walk, which is normally 'four-beat' with each foot falling at a different tempo. An ape uses a four-beat walk.

2. The trot, a 'two-beat' gait where diagonal legs (right front/left hind, left front/right hind) fall at the same time. A horse's trot is similar to a dog's.

3. The gallop, or run, which will vary considerably by species. A horse's gallop is completely different from a dog's.

4. Some animals, such as bears, will 'pace' by moving two legs on the same side of the body in a two-beat gait.

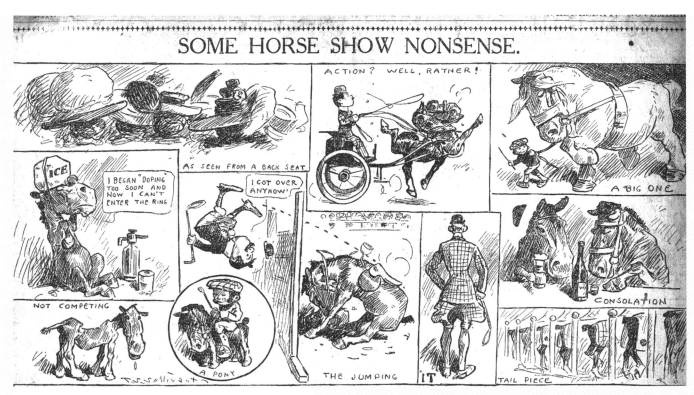

4.1

Animal caricature

T. S. Sullivant's animal caricatures acted like humans but never lost their animal qualities.

Illustration by T. S. Sullivant, 1903

4.2

Animated animals with human qualities

Animated animals have demonstrated human qualities ever since Winsor McCay's 1914 cartoon *Gertie the Dinosaur*. Gertie cried when scolded by her trainer in the first animated film to portray an animated character's emotions and personality.

Courtesy of MCCAY/The Kobal Collection

Four legs good, two legs better? Creating animal characters

FIG. I.

FIG. II.

"The Monkey" by T.S. Sullivant
JUDGE magazine, 1912

FIG. IV.

Newspaper heading,
1903

T. S. Sullivant, "Life" magazine, 1921

"We'll all look like that some day, Willie."
"And you too, Aunt Martha?"

4.3

Apes

Apes, our closest relatives, have pelvises and spines that put
them firmly in the quadruped camp – very different from our
bipedal skeletal structure.
Illustrations by T. S. Sullivant (1903, 1912, 1921)

4.4

All fours

Adult humans find it difficult to walk on all fours.

Illustration 'All Fours' © 2008 by Simon Ward-Horner

4.5

Quadruped gaits

The walk, trot, and gallop/run are standard quadruped gaits, though they will not be performed identically by all animals due to differences in their skeletal construction and weight.

4.6

A crawling infant

A crawling infant will move like a quadruped on hands and knees.

Four legs good, two legs better? Creating animal characters

Performing animals

Animator Ellen Woodbury is an expert in animal and bird animation. She worked at the Walt Disney Animation Studios as supervising animator/designer on Zazu in *The Lion King* (1994), Pegasus in *Hercules* (1997), and various alien pirates in *Treasure Planet* (2002). I discussed two of Ellen's characters with her in an online interview in 2009. This section is left in her own words since she needs no interpretation.

Ellen Woodbury: An animator should learn all the 'standard' gaits of a four-legged animal if he or she is going to animate one. Then the animator needs to learn the textures and shapes of their specific animal of choice. A pig moves a lot differently than a cat even though they may both be doing a four-beat walk, and you need to animate each animal true to their own way of going. If an animator wants to achieve sincerity in their work, he or she needs to come from a smart place. Do your homework – study the animal live and in person. Shoot reference footage and single-frame through it. Study other film/video materials made by other people. Find as many pictures as you can in books that show your animal doing their daily activities, or extraordinary activities. If possible, find the real animal that you can touch to feel the texture of their skin or fur. Pick up their feet, feel their bones through the skin. Get to know them.... In studying footage of the animal, draw thumbnails of all the extremes and breakdowns. Pay attention to the range of each joint (how big their arcs of movement are) and how and when (what part of the stride) they shift their weight.

Some animals are very stiff, like goats and horses. Some animals are very loose-jointed, like cats.... As an animator, you want your audience to believe in your character whether he or she is broad and cartoony or realistic. The more characteristics and nuances you can put into your animal character's performance, the richer you make it, and the more your audience is going to want to believe in him or her. Research pays off. Once you know the basic three gaits of your particular animal, you need to shoot some footage of your animal playing. When animals play, they move freely, mix up their foot patterns, shift their weight all over the place – just like people when they play. Thumbnail all the moves that look interesting to you and gradually you will catch on to the rhythms, angles, flexibility and textures of the animal. It is like learning a new language, but in movement. Remember that all of the above is just mechanics. When you add in the personality of the animal character is when it gets really exciting and fun.

Q: Chuck Jones mentioned that every horse moves the same way, but every human moves differently. Was he correct?

Ellen Woodbury: Yes and no. Basic gaits in a horse have the same foot pattern. A walk has four beats – the hind foot steps into or near the footprint of the front foot just picked up on the same side. The trot is a two-beat gait with diagonal pairs working together. That is the 'yes' part that Chuck Jones was talking about. Here's my two cents (the 'no' part). Given that there are basic gaits, I argue (as would any person familiar with horses) that every single horse moves differently than every other horse. Some are stiff and short-strided; some are fluid, flamboyant, and flashy, with huge arcs in their leg joints. Some horses naturally carry their heads very high, and some carry their heads very low. Body composition of different breeds influences differences in movement, just like in dogs. Combine the appropriate nuances in movement with the particular personality of your horse character and you will have a different-moving horse every time.

100 4. ANIMAL ACTORS

Four legs good, two legs better? Creating animal characters · Flights of imagination: Animating winged characters >

Q: You once told me that Eadweard Muybridge's photographic studies of the movement of horses and riders were now hopelessly out of date and that we ride differently now. What has changed since Muybridge's day, and how may an animator who is not a horseman research this action today?

Ellen Woodbury: At the turn of the 20th century (Muybridge's time) people rode in more of a *chair seat*, with their feet out in front of them. Today, people ride with their legs under their bodies – the line-up of body parts varies such as shoulder-hip-heel or knees and toes, and so on. The best way to know this is to take riding lessons yourself, and watch other riders in different disciplines such as western, hunter, jumper, dressage, and so on. By watching, you teach your brain to see the differences. By riding, your body learns the differences. Muscular memory is part of animating from a smart place. If you know in your own body what an action feels like, you can look at your animation and determine if it feels right.

– Ellen Woodbury interview with Nancy Beiman (2009)

A well-animated quadruped will maintain some of the original creature's qualities of motion and timing leavened with a reasonable amount of poetic licence. An artistic *impression* of the animal is much more effective in animation than a literal depiction of its movement.

When He Hired Him for a Quiet Ride He Didn't Know He Was "Snow Flake, the Educated Equine Wonder."

4.7

When he hired him for a quiet ride he didn't know he was 'Snow Flake, the Educated Equine Wonder'.
A quadruped animal's arc of movement depends on its muscular and skeletal construction. Animators and cartoonists will base caricatured action on observations of reality.
Drawing by A. B. Frost (1922)

Four legs good, two legs better? Creating animal characters

Feeling your way

Rather than stating that 'that action *looks* like a cat' animators will say, 'that action *feels* like a cat'. This is because we are describing an impression created by a series of moving drawings rather than analysing a single static image. The word '*feeling*' is used to describe all textures, whether animated or static. For instance, a piece of animated cloth may not be touched, but it can be 'felt'! (The pun is intentional.) We feel the texture of the animated character's movement in the same way.

In Chapter 2 we saw how variable timing of primary and secondary actions and overlap in different parts of the animated figure creates texture in animation timing. Texture in *drawing* or *posing* varies the tension in different parts of a character's body to create the feeling that it is composed of different materials. For example, a cat's soft fur and loose skin cover a muscular body and some prominent bones that show on the surface of all but a very obese animal. Chuck Jones once amusingly described a cat as 'a bag' whose contents settled when the creature sat and stretched out when it moved. Other textures may be involved. An artist may create the *feel* of fur and bone by varying the weight and shape of the line, playing curved shapes against straight ones, and stretching or compressing parts of the cat's body.

4.8

The *feel* of fur and bone
The photographs show the tremendous flexibility of my cat Gizmo's body. My drawings indicate the soft feel of Gizmo's fur and the hardness of the underlying bone by varying line textures and volumes.

102 4. ANIMAL ACTORS

Four legs good, two legs better? Creating animal characters · Flights of imagination: Animating winged characters >

4.9

Humanising animals

In this illustration, Gizmo and her escorts Buddy and Roswell, are humanised and dressed in period costume, without losing all of their 'cat' qualities. They walk on tiptoe, as real cats do, on their hind legs. Photographs of Gizmo and life drawings of Buddy and Roswell served as reference for the caricature. This type of humanised animal caricature is common in animation.

Illustration © 2008 by Nina Haley.

4.10

Animal body language

Like humans, an animal will show its emotional state through its body language. For example, my cat Gizmo appears relaxed and happy in the first photograph. She is slightly more reserved in the second.

Four legs good, two legs better? Creating animal characters

Animation by association

Animated acting goes beyond realism. We are creating the *feel* of the animal rather than literally recreating its movements. I often analyse the action of more than one animal species when animating a specific creature. Designers call this 'association'. It's a good word for animators to use as well.

Artist Rico LeBrun drew a 64-page guide to the *Skeleton Action of the Deer* for the Walt Disney Studio during the production of *Bambi* (1942). LeBrun peppered his pages with wonderful thumbnails showing how the feel of the deer's action might be associated with ballet dancers, people walking on crutches and stilts, drunks, boxers, skaters, an accordion and even Charlie Chaplin. These associations were used when Bambi is learning to walk and in the famous sequence where he and Thumper play on ice.

Let's try some association. A cat's movements are often described as 'fluid'. I've seen my cat Gizmo squeeze effortlessly through a two-inch wide gap in a window for all the world like toothpaste squeezing out of a tube. A cat's body is extremely flexible. What other animal has this quality? The 'feeling' of a snake, or toothpaste, or both together, can be incorporated into the animation of a cat to intensify 'cat' qualities in much the same way that a little salt is added to a cake recipe to intensify sweetness.

Here is a list of the qualities (animal, vegetable, and inanimate) that I associate with the feel of a cat's movements:

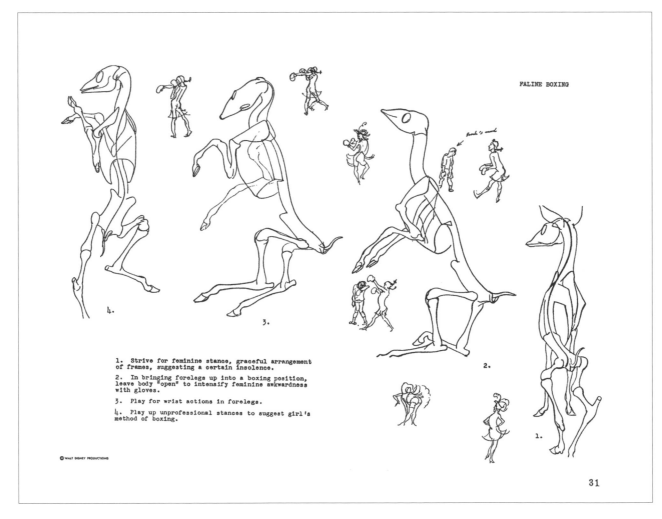

FALINE BOXING

1. Strive for feminine stance, graceful arrangement of frames, suggesting a certain insolence.

2. In bringing forelegs up into a boxing position, leave body "open" to intensify feminine awkwardness with gloves.

3. Play for wrist actions in forelegs.

4. Play up unprofessional stances to suggest girl's method of boxing.

© WALT DISNEY PRODUCTIONS

31

4.11
Skeleton action of the deer
Rico LeBrun's thumbnail illustrations in *Skeleton Action of the Deer* (1935) compare caricatured animal and human motion. The realistic skeletons perform actions that 'real' deer cannot.
©Disney Enterprises, Inc.

- Snake
- Fish (a small, darting one like a neon tetra)
- Fluid (semi-congealed, like toothpaste)
- Clinging vine
- Rubber band
- Coiled spring
- Whip
- Steel trap
- Cigarette smoke

What might happen when the *feel* of these materials are incorporated into the animation of a cat?

The cat's emotional state will have a major influence on the 'feel' of the action. In the scenes shown in Fig. 4.12 and Fig. 4.14, the cat's emotions range from curiosity to fear. This transition is handled texturally – it happens gradually, not all at once. I may 'act out' the movement using only my hands (since hands and fingers are the most flexible part of the human body) to block the action and set the timing. I label or shade portions of each drawing to describe the different textures in the cat's body and how they feel. These will not be consistent: a 'soft' area in one pose may feel tense in the next one.

The resulting scene is a performance that is unique to the animator, rather than a mere action analysis exercise.

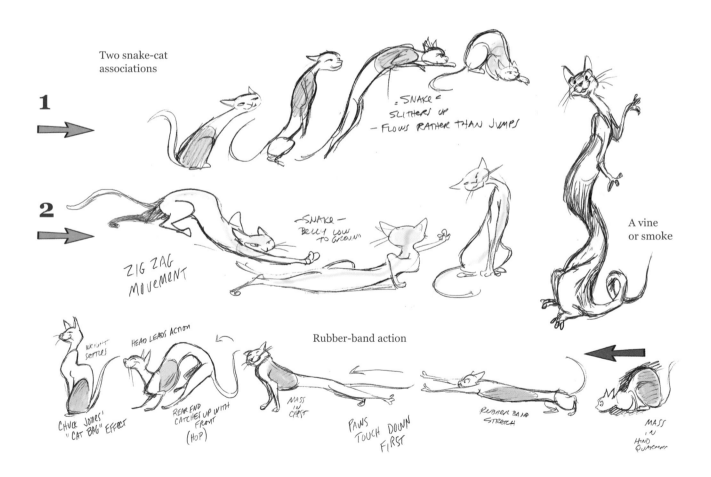

4.12

Feline movements and characteristics

A cat's movements and characteristics can be suggested by other animals or substances. A quality may apply to only one part of the cat's movement; thumbnails are labelled so that these associations may be translated into the animated scene.

List other animals or substances with characteristics that can create the feel of these quadrupedal animals in action.

Write the animal names and your associations on a separate piece of paper. Then draw two or three action thumbnails for each association, combining the item's qualities with the animal's movements. Choose the association that works best for you and animate a brief action test (a simple cycle or action that is not more than five seconds long) on one of the animals. Does the result give you a stronger 'feeling' than you would have if you only referenced the original animal?

1. Elephant

Association: _____

2. Giraffe

Association: _____

3. Monkey

Association: _____

4. Turtle

Association: _____

5. Bear

Association: _____

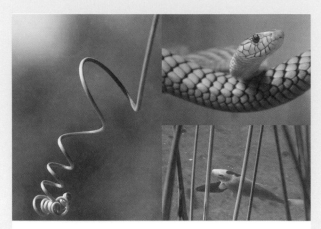

4.13

Associated materials
I associate these materials and animals with the feel of a cat's movements rather than its appearance.
Photos courtesy of PDPhoto.org

Slightly more 'realistic' caricature of cat action

Associations   meatloaf or bread...   liquid kitty   tail overlaps around   meatball

4.14

A unique performance
Textures, associations, and emotions combine to create a unique performance.

Talking animals

Animal mouth shapes will vary considerably since you will be dealing with projecting muzzles, beaks, trunks, and snouts. Soft textures such as pig snouts will animate easily, but a hard beak poses problems. How does a bird create the 'oo' mouth shape without lips?

A bit of softening is often necessary to create the feeling of 'cartoon cartilage' (an amusing term described by Ellen Woodbury in the next section of this chapter). The softness will vary by species and body part and must be handled on a case-by-case basis. Animated muzzles will stretch and assume shapes that are impossible for the actual creature to perform, but the distortion will be less extreme than that of the softer areas such as flesh and fur. Over-distortion can give a 'rubbery' or 'mushy' quality to the animation. Talking animals can show or grow teeth when needed to help with their pronunciation. (Even birds will sometimes have teeth.) A projecting muzzle, like a beak, will become elastic 'cartoon cartilage' during speech but must still make us believe that it is part of the animal's skull.

4.15

Muzzles and mouths
Talking animals' muzzles and mouths are composed of 'cartoon cartilage' that distorts while maintaining believability.

4 Animal actors

Four legs good, two legs better? Creating animal characters

Violent distortion works
when it returns to
'normal' proportions

a

Volume control

Animators often break or violently distort a character's muzzle, jaw, or entire head for expressions or dialogue mouths if the scene calls for it. The illusion of a solid skull and figure will be maintained if the distorted mouth or body part returns to the original volume afterwards, just as a bouncing ball resumes its original shape when not affected by outside forces. Some character designs are more conducive to distortion than others; your story, character designs, and artistic philosophy will determine just 'how far you can go' with distortion. Figure 4.16 a and b show examples of a violently distorted 'graphic' character and a rounded character with some slight distortion. There is no right or wrong way to animate these changes; there is only the way that works best for your scene and your project.

You can keep character volumes consistent by keeping a normally proportioned drawing of the character's face and body underneath your animation keys if you are animating on paper. These are known as 'character layouts', and a new one should be drawn for each scene since the acting and size of the character will vary with the staging. The character layout pose can also be drawn directly on a tablet or scanned in and kept on the desktop if you are working digitally.

This will minimise morphing, growing or shrinking volumes, and 'evolution' of the character design as you animate the scene, and help to maintain the character's believability.

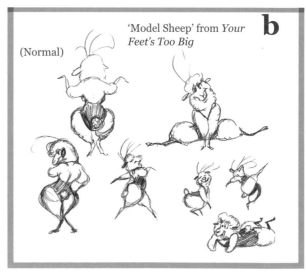

(Normal)

'Model Sheep' from *Your Feet's Too Big*

b

4.16 a and b

Reference drawings help avoid over-distortion
Over-distortion can result in a rubbery feeling or *'mushiness'* in the animation. A reference drawing of the character (character layout) helps the animator maintain volumes and design consistency in each scene.
© Nancy Beiman

The master's thumbs:
Frank Thomas and Eric Larson

Frank Thomas recommended that quadruped animals who must act while walking or running have the body and head action blocked in first, with legs added afterwards. He used this technique when animating Bambi. The body and head are the primary action and the legs are secondary action, although Frank would modify the body as needed if the legs were exerting unequal forces on the bodies.

Eric Larson described a diametrically opposed principle in one sentence that has never left me: 'The legs furnish the power.' In other words, Eric would animate his animals from the 'ground up', blocking the legs first (influencing the body movement) as primary action, and possibly use secondary action on the head.

I have usually worked Eric's way since knowing where the character's feet are gives a wonderful, solid weight to all your animation even in medium close-ups. Frank's system is equally effective, particularly in dialogue scenes. You may use Frank's or Eric's method or a combination of the two. Let the circumstances of the scene and the character of the animal dictate your method of working. When animating cats I blocked head, legs, and body together. The tail, ears, and whiskers were secondary action. There is no standard method. Animate what you *feel*. Use any technique that 'will fly'.

Body first   (Frank Thomas' method)

Feet first   (Eric Larson's method)

4.17

Thumbnailing styles

The characteristics of the animal and the requirements of each scene will affect your acting style. Frank Thomas' and Eric Larson's thumbnailing styles are equally effective.

Next >

Next, we'll consider some creatures that DO fly.

Flights of imagination: Animating winged characters

'It is not only fine feathers that make fine birds.'

– Aesop

Birds are technically quadruped animals with extensively modified fore limbs that move in a vastly different manner from the hind limbs. Their movements are influenced by their environment. Birds can move easily through two elements: water (for example, a swimming penguin or duck) and air. Birds move less efficiently on the ground although one flightless bird, the ostrich, can run faster than a greyhound!

Even when flying, birds do not have 'standard' gaits like other quadrupeds. Flight methods vary considerably depending on the species. An albatross glides, a pigeon flutters and a hawk soars. A hummingbird's rapidly beating wing gives its flight a completely different quality from that of a swallow or an owl. Bird *species*, rather than *gaits*, must be analysed individually when creating animated avian characters.

As we've already seen, animator Ellen Woodbury is an expert in animal and bird animation and I discussed two of Ellen's characters with her online early in 2009. This section is in Ellen's own words and provides an excellent insight into her working methods and thought processes.

Mr Bean as Mr Bird: Zazu in *The Lion King* (1992)

Q: What sort of research did you undertake to create Zazu's moves? What percentage was based on voice actor Rowan Atkinson and what percentage on a 'real' hornbill?

Ellen Woodbury: For Zazu, I researched hornbills initially. There is very little footage of hornbills doing everyday things. Mostly, I found documentaries about how they build their nests in holes in tree trunks, and then the male walls the female into the nest with mud to keep the female, eggs and subsequent chicks safe from snakes. (Not a lot there I could use for Zazu.) The directors shot some reference footage of hornbills hopping around on the ground on their research trip to Africa, which was quite useful. Also, Jim Fowler brought a hornbill with him to our studio when we had a massive animal-research study period before production started on *The Lion King*. That was also very helpful.

After studying the hornbills, I studied all kinds of birds, concentrating on those the size of crows (close to the size of Zazu in the film) for wing arcs when flying. I then looked at landings and take-offs of all kinds of birds. I studied how they ate, how they walked around and the tick-tock way their tails move, the textures of their head turns and twitches. During the same time, I looked at every bit of footage I could find on Rowan Atkinson. His series *Blackadder* (1983–1989) was a particularly rich source for me.

4.18

Zazu's walk

'This works out the walk as Zazu approaches Mufasa. I want to overlap the head in the first sigh. I try to time the scene out in thumbnails to see how close I can get to what I want on the first throw-down pass.'

– Ellen Woodbury

Frame numbers (approximate) and dialogue are written on the thumbnails to set rough timing.

The Lion King artwork © Disney Enterprises inc.

Then I wrote down the characteristics of Zazu, which were evident in the storyline of *The Lion King's* script. Zazu is loyal, traditional, takes pride in his job as the king's majordomo, dislikes children, and so on. Then I brainstormed from my research and grabbed ideas and started putting them together. Zazu is proud – real hornbills sometimes stand with their chests puffed out in a proud-looking posture. They hop deliberately and with a force to their landings, a bit huffy and superior. I could use that for Zazu. Rowan Atkinson has a malleable face, a huge range of expressions – I took that and added it to Zazu. Rowan played Zazu *spitting out* his words – that works with the huffy postures and deliberate actions. I gathered information, sorted through it, and edited until I had my character.

Q: How much distortion did you use on Zazu's beak during his dialogue? (I am thinking of scenes where Zazu's mouth is an *'oo'* shape, which is impossible to obtain with a 'real' beak.)

Ellen Woodbury: All the characters I have animated are composed of *'cartoon cartilage'*, not bone. The fleshy parts are, of course, soft and squashy. The hard parts are always flexible to a point... not hard and stiff. If Zazu's beak were not made of 'cartoon cartilage' he could never talk convincingly, and that would be a tragedy because Zazu *loves* to talk. Part of the fun and believability of animated characters is watching them talk. I experimented with Zazu's beak and took it as far as I could without it getting mushy, keeping the feeling that it was a stiff material but not so stiff that I sacrificed the entertainment and credibility of him speaking.

4.19
Mr Bean
Actor Rowan Atkinson's appearance was caricatured in Zazu's design.
Polygram/The Kobal Collection/Hanover, Suzanne

4.20
Zazu's line
Several interpretations of Zazu's line, 'In *mine*, actually!' were thumbnailed for this dialogue scene. 'I put all my thoughts down in thumbnails so it frees up my mind on the first rough pass... so I can "plus" (improve) on what is here.'
– Ellen Woodbury
The Lion King artwork © Disney Enterprises Inc.

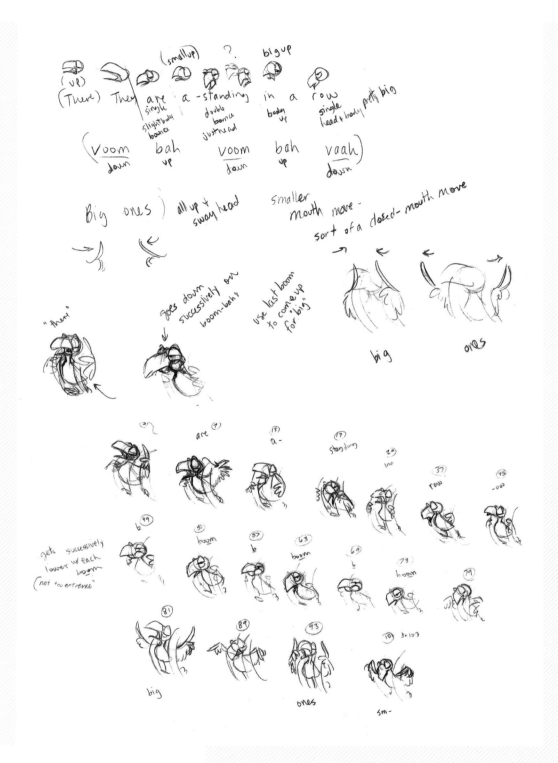

4.21

'I've got a Luverly Bunch of Cokernuts.'

'Thumbnails from the "ribcage scene" where Zazu sings
'I've Got a Luverly Bunch of Cokernuts'. The first thumbnails
analyse the track and have my first ideas for the acting.
Then I refine and rebuild the ideas fully. Lines under letters
in words indicate which letter goes with a pose.'

– Ellen Woodbury

The Lion King artwork © Disney Enterprises Inc.

Flights of imagination: Animating winged characters

A horse of a different colour:
Pegasus in Disney's *Hercules* (1997)

Q: Pegasus combines characteristics of two different animals. Is he more horse than bird, or vice versa? Do his avian/equine proportions and characteristics change depending on the situation?

Ellen Woodbury: When I first started working on Pegasus I already had a lot of knowledge of birds from my research for Zazu. I studied large birds for this character because I wanted to preserve the feeling of weight in a big horse. I also had a lot of horse knowledge as I have been an enthusiastic rider and horse-owner for most of my life. I took notes about how Pegasus was presented in the script. I talked with the directors (John Musker and Ron Clements) about their vision for Pegasus' personality. I brainstormed bird and horse behaviours. Peg is also a jock, so I researched athletes and football training tapes as well. A friend taught me how to make a proper fist and throw a punch – I was suddenly interested in jock culture.

Peg is 100 per cent horse *and* bird. He is an amalgam of my research, direction from Ron (Clements) and John (Musker), his role in the story and relationships to Herc, Meg, and Phil. My main starting point in developing Peg was Zeus' line, 'He's a magnificent horse with the brain of a bird.' Let your imagination go and see where it takes you!

The write stuff: Consolidating your ideas

Like an actor, the animator has to keep their actions 'in character'. If your project is adapting a story from another medium, such as *Treasure Planet* (2002) *or The Hunchback of Notre Dame* (1996) the original material gives the animator some guidelines to follow. In the case of *Hercules*, Pegasus was not only a winged horse – he was a bit of a 'jock', almost a caricature of Hercules. Ellen first drew a very rough size comparison of Hercules and Pegasus, since they worked together for most of the picture. Some notes that she 'brainstormed' early on in the creative process are shown on page 115. Not all these qualities will be literally portrayed on screen, but they offer the animator(s) an insight into Pegasus' mind and suggest motivation for his actions.

TIP

Simple, accessible and concise

You do not need to write a lengthy 'back story' for an animated character. Ellen's bullet points suggest Pegasus' basic motivation and possible action. These points will guide her animation. The list of behaviours is like a paint palette. A varying mixture of emotional 'colours' can illustrate how the character responds in different situations. (The response might be influenced by another character, as when Pegasus shows his dislike of Megaera.) Events that occur prior to the start of the film – say, Pegasus' relationship with his mother – are not relevant in this instance. This is not always the case, but background notes for an animated character should be simple, accessible and concise.

Pegasus' personality:

* Heart of gold, brain of a bird. He is physical; he invades others' physical space.

* Honest, innocent, athletic jock; conceited, fearless, confident, silly and loyal.

* Wide-eyed, enthusiastic, dumb and friendly.

* His neutral attitude is friendly/happy.

* Agreeable, good-natured, childlike. Can't stand still. Emotions are up front and obvious. Quick responses are not thought out. Team mentality. Lots of pent-up energy; over-energised.

* (He is a) caricature of Herc, in naïveté and enthusiasm.

Team mentality: He laughs at Herc. Jock competitiveness, all in fun.

Childlike: Short attention span. Over-energised, messing around and snooping in everything. Active. Does what he wants, even though asked or told not to. Forgets he was told not to do something. Catalyst for Herc – infectious goofing around.

Relationship: (Pegasus) likes Phil (Philoctetes the satyr) because he is part animal. Phil is not crazy about him. He relates to Phil as an animal, which Phil doesn't like.

Loves Herc (Hercules) like a brother. Sibling rivalry, jealousy, jock competitiveness, laughs at Herc to razz him. An emotional caricature of Herc – ultra-dense, innocent, exuberant.

Hates Meg (Megaera, Hercules' girlfriend) because she is butting in on their 'buddy thing'. Has no idea what she is talking about. He annoys her as much as possible and it is like a game or competition to him.

(Pegasus) will chew on someone's hand, clothing, personal possessions and leave them all slobbery… step on someone's foot, pretending not to notice.

Bird behaviour

* Preening

* Flying stuff – swoops, power dives, loop de loops, hovers, free fall

* Bird bath

* Eating bird seed

* Hopping

* Perching on people and objects

* Tweeting

* Quick head turns and short attention span

* Nesting

* Sitting on eggs

* Pecking and scratching in dirt

Horse behaviour

* Using people and objects for scratching post

* Banging into people or walking over or through them, generally throwing his weight around

* Blows his nose into someone's face

* Presents his butt to someone when he disagrees with them

* Scrounges around in someone's hair with his nose

* Slaps someone with his tail

Ellen Woodbury

The equine athlete

Q: Did you base Pegasus on athletes, or give him the qualities of this type of human?

Ellen Woodbury: As I mentioned above, I studied football training tapes to learn how jocks and teammates relate to each other. They were incredibly physical, bashing into each other – this is where the business with the head butts came from: two football players leap into the air towards each other and crash their helmets together right between the eyes in mid-air. Ah yes, I had another dimension to my character.

Q: I remember that you originally had no 'dialogue' track read for Peg before you started animating. Could you possibly have animated this character 'silent' and allowed them to add the horse noises in the post-production mix? Or was it essential for Pegasus to have the same track treatment (sound recorded and read prior to animation) as 'speaking' characters?

Ellen Woodbury: Peg's noises, though not dialogue, needed to be read [*broken down phonetically*] on the x-sheet. Knowing the frame where the emphasis falls on a syllable, even though it is just part of a whinny or little chirps, is absolutely necessary if you are going to make that sound feel and look like it is coming out of the character.... Animation, particularly Disney animation, is all about creating and sustaining the illusion. We went to enormous lengths to create environments in our films with the appropriate perspectives and textures, and dimensional personalities for characters who move with believable weight and timing such that we, and the audience, could believe in them. It was our responsibility as animators to sustain that illusion and do everything we could to entice the audience to buy into our fantastic realities. Putting a sound-over on Pegasus defeats the purpose of creating that illusion.

4.22

Affection from Pegasus
'He will chew on someone's hand, clothing, and personal possessions and leave them all slobbery...'
Ellen Woodbury
Hercules artwork © Disney Enterprises Inc.

116 4. ANIMAL ACTORS

< Four legs good, two legs better? Creating animal characters · <u>Flights of imagination: Animating winged characters</u> · Portraying animal qualities in human characters >

4.23

Getting started

'I start with my ideas and directors' notes from the hand-out
meeting. I then analyse the soundtrack for accents. I act it
out with the track until I get what I want. Then I 'script' the
scene with the soundtrack, if it is complicated, like in this
scene. Both Andreas Deja (the *Hercules* lead) and I met with
the directors and went through these (thumbnails).'

– Ellen Woodbury. *Hercules* artwork © Disney Enterprises Inc.

Flights of imagination: Animating winged characters

Ellen Woodbury: I put great value in thumbnails as a way to plan a scene. Imagination must play a large part in acting out a scene, particularly if you are animating something dangerous. I learn enough to have the movement play in my head the way I want it, then thumbnail, then do a first rough pass (the throw-down) and shoot a test to see if it works – if the movement on the screen loops with my feeling about the move in my imagination and I am in synch with my animation, I tweak and modify from there until the scene works for me.

4.24

Pegasus puff

'Pegasus "puffs" the centaur Nessus over. The mouth action is extensively thumbnailed, but is impossible for an actual horse to perform.'

Hercules artwork © Disney Enterprises inc.

< Four legs good, two legs better? Creating animal characters · Flights of imagination: Animating winged characters · Portraying animal qualities in human characters >

4.2 Analyse and sketch

➤ Analyse and sketch the action of a specific bird species. You may draw from life or use a nature DVD (several suggestions appear on page 125). Capture the motion and silhouette of the bird – don't be distracted by feather patterns and colours.

➤ After you have done this, draw about a dozen thumbnail poses of the bird in various emotional attitudes. Review the 'emotion' exercise with Sam in Chapter 1 for some suggestions if you need them.

➤ Then thumbnail or animate a short scene of the bird walking or flying while expressing one of the emotions. How might a chicken move when it is angry? How does an ostrich show sadness?

➤ Next, try combining the bird's action and emotion with that of a human being. Draw thumbnails of a human in specific emotions and attitudes (you may analyse an actor's filmed performance, or you can sketch people from life).

➤ Draw new thumbnails of the bird that incorporate the human's emotions and characteristic gestures.

Next >

In the next section we will consider how the animation of human beings might portray a little of their 'Inner Beast'.

Portraying animal qualities in human characters

'If man could be crossed with the cat it would improve man, but it would deteriorate the cat.'

– Mark Twain, *Notebook* (1894)

The animated human is traditionally the most difficult character to perform since we see human beings every day, starting with our own reflection in the bathroom mirror. We know how humans are supposed to move. Any acting slip-ups, strangeness of proportion, or lack of solidity in the animation of a human character will be instantly noticed. The audience is more forgiving when viewing animated animal or fantasy characters.

Some animated humans are 'associated' with non-human characteristics. They move, behave, and even physically resemble animals that symbolise their inner thoughts or personalities. Think of the vulture-like Cruella de Ville and her crow-like followers the Bad'uns in *One Hundred and One Dalmatians* (Walt Disney Productions, 1961). The villains are ostensibly human, but their acting suggests 'the beast within'.

This section will discuss human characters that suggest, rather than literally embody, animals when acting. Literal human/animal combinations will be discussed in Chapter 5.

Downward dogs: Negative animal symbolism

Humans are often compared to animals in a derogatory sense but an animal can symbolise both positive and negative human qualities. Robert Louis Stevenson described the odious Mr Hyde's rages as 'ape-like' in *Dr Jekyll and Mr Hyde* (1886). But Tarzan and his ape 'mother', Kala, demonstrated a touching mother-son relationship that was as powerful as a human's in Edgar Rice Burroughs' *Tarzan of the Apes* (1918).

A great many negative references are associated with the face and head. People can be *fish-, horse-,* or *rat-faced, piggy-eyed* or *turkey-necked*. Human personalities are also sometimes described as *catty, sheepish, hangdog,* and the ever-popular *chicken*. Your character's design can reflect these descriptions (and what fine visuals they conjure up!) But why stop at the appearance? What if the character animation continued the design's animal similes?

A *rat-faced* man might scurry or scamper through life with his body held relatively low to the ground like his namesake. This can be more interesting than having him perform a standard cycle run based on purely human action. A *fish-faced* character might have popping eyes, an adenoidal voice, a mouth that frequently hangs open, and a flat-footed walk. These qualities may or may not be an outward depiction of Fish-face or Rat-face's moral character. Animated acting can portray the 'animal soul' of a human character – but the story context will cast them as heroes or villains. They may be decent people even though their looks are against them. Quasimodo, the Hunchback of Notre Dame, has a grotesque appearance (frequently compared to a beast's) that is countered by his noble inner nature. On the other hand, Mr Burns from *The Simpsons* (1989–present) is a rat-faced man whose soul is as contorted as his posture.

4.25

Animal qualities – so many are possible!
Human characters may suggest animal qualities in their movement and design.

4.3 Human/animal association

➤ Analyse a live-action motion picture film of a human in action, ideally from a motion picture with a linear story. You may want to use a well-known actor or actress' performance for this exercise. Sketch key poses of the actor's body in motion. Work rough; do not try to draw a literal representation of the actor. You may use caricature elements if desired.

➤ Now consider which animal the actor or actress' movement might suggest. The species may be symbolic (a king portrayed as a lion). It need not resemble the actor, but should associate with his/her performance so as to intensify the existing emotions. You may also try using a contrasting animal (for example, a rabbit with a large, villainous actor).

➤ Next, find some live-action footage of the animal (unless you have access to a real one) and draw quick sketches based on the creature's movements.

➤ Lastly, do 'association' sketches combining the animal's poses with that of the human. Do not combine them equally; keep the figure human, but suggest the animal in body attitudes and movement. You may add a few beastly details to the face. List the basic emotions that the character might portray or write one or two sentences of story context before sketching your character.

➤ Try thumbnailing a second version that associates the same human with a different animal. How does this vary your perception of the character?

➤ Pick the combination that works best for you. Thumbnail a bipedal walk cycle in which the animal's movements are associated with the human. Shoot a pose test afterward and adjust the timing as needed. Finish the animated scene if desired.

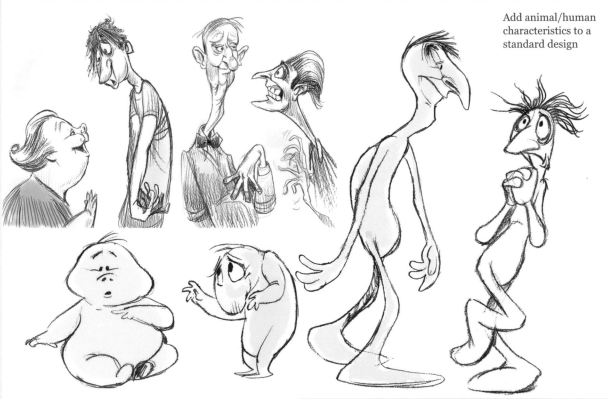

Add animal/human characteristics to a standard design

4.26

Animal/human caricatures
Match the animal names with the human caricatures:
Piggy-eyed, turkey-necked, sheepish and chicken.

Take the human character from Exercise 4.3 and redesign it with some of the **negative animal qualities** in the following lists. You can combine one or more of the animal characteristics if you like.

Rat-faced	Catty
Piggy-eyed	Jackass
Turkey-necked	Dog-like
Chicken-legs	Sheepish
Horse-faced	Slothful

Now draw several rough poses of this new character design performing the following actions, using a **positive** interpretation of its personality. Use suitable props.

➤ Baking a cake

➤ Picking a bunch of flowers

➤ Dancing

Analyse the results and answer the following questions (discuss them with a friend, or write the answers on a separate piece of paper.)

➤ Do you find it difficult to portray **positive** actions with this character?

➤ Does your character's body language reflect its **appearance**, or its **inner being**?

After you have analysed the drawings, proceed to Exercise 4.5.

Sketch the character from Exercise 4.4 in the same situations, using the negative interpretation of its personality. Then consider these questions:

➤ Did you use more of the 'animal' qualities in the **negative** interpretation?

➤ Were the same props used in the two approaches?

➤ Was it easier to portray the negative character?

Positive animal characteristics

Positive animalistic qualities can be incorporated into human characters' actions. A lovely woman might move like a cat or a butterfly; an innocent child might move in a manner that suggests a rabbit or mouse while a not-very-nice child may resemble a rat. (Yes, there are nice rats too.) Of course the story will ultimately determine which animal qualities you might associate with the human characters.

Getting in touch with the inner 'Beast' can bring a lot of 'Beauty' to animated humans and create a unique performance.

4.27

Dialogue mouths
Dialogue mouths will be influenced by the soundtrack, depending on whether they 'hiss', 'purr', 'roar', 'snarl', 'chatter', 'whine' or even 'bark'. You may reference more than one species of animal for different movements or mouth shapes on your character.

TIP
Dialogue variations

Animal associations can strongly influence mouth shapes. Human characters can snarl, bark, croak, purr, or hiss their lines. Experiment with your interpretations. The dialogue will create the association; you might reference more than one animal in your performance. Keep your characters and your interpretations loose and flexible; as Disney director Jack Hannah once told me, 'It is a lot easier to go a little farther (into caricature) than required and tone it down a bit than to not go far enough and try to exaggerate the poses afterward.'

4.28

Positive characteristics
A man, woman and child with their animal equivalents.

DVD Reference: Animal characters

There are many excellent films featuring animal characters that move like animals and act like humans. Far fewer films have humans behaving like animals. Here are a few suggestions for viewing.

The Gold Rush (1925) In the cabin sequence Charlie Chaplin fights off a starving, bear-like prospector who believes that Charlie has turned into a chicken.

Bambi (1942) The behaviour of the young deer, rabbit, and skunk is partly based on the actions and expressions of human children. Thumper continues to show 'human' actions and emotions after he matures, but Bambi and Faline outgrow it.

Cinderella (1950) Ward Kimball's animation of Lucifer the Cat associates snake and feline movements. Kimball's Siamese cat animation in *Lady and the Tramp* (1955) incorporates the movement of Balinese dancers.

The Ladykillers (1955, Ealing Studios) The villains in this dark comedy resemble cats or rats; the sweet little old ladies who defeat them are associated with parrots. Watch for animal and bird associations in movement (Alec Guinness' 'Professor' advances on a parrot with his hand extended like a cat's paw), colour (the old ladies wear pink and white, matching the cockatoo's feathers), and even sound (Mrs Wilberforce repeats everything that she is told).

One Hundred and One Dalmatians (1961) Cruella de Ville and her villainous Bad'uns resemble vultures and crows in their design and movement. Cruella's shadow darkens the door before she enters exactly as Alec Guinness' did in *The Ladykillers*.

The Jungle Book (1967) Milt Kahl's animation of Shere Khan the tiger beautifully associates the attitudes and expressions of voice actor George Sanders with the cat's movements. Ollie Johnston's wonderful Kaa the snake grows 'arms' for expression or turns into a graphic symbol when it is appropriate for the action. Mowgli the human imitates the movements of bear, ape, elephant, and monkey characters.

Allegro Non Troppo (1977) The Valse Triste sequence features a beautifully animated cat that blends some mercurial, or liquid, elements with the feline.

The Lion King (1994) Ellen Woodbury's animation of Zazu blends caricatures of the hornbill and voice actor Rowan Atkinson.

The Triplets of Belleville (2003) Bruno the dog is a beautifully analysed portrayal of an old, overweight mutt that is pure 'dog'.

Guard Dog, Guide Dog, and Hot Dog (2004-2008) by Bill Plympton feature a stylised and very funny bulldog character.

Simon's Cat (2008-present) by Simon Tofield is a beautiful depiction of feline personality and action.

Famous Fred (1996) by Joanna Quinn caricatures a feline Elvis Presley with a supporting cast of cats, children and a guinea pig with a bad back.

Next >

We will next consider creatures that may have great acting potential even if they may find it impossible to *'break a leg'*.

'Look Ma, no hands!' Animating snakes, worms, and other crawlers

'You must crawl before you can walk.'

– Folk saying

Consider two parallel lines isolated on a sea of paper. It isn't possible to determine what they are made of, or whether they are meant to represent a two- or three-dimensional shape. They are simply two lines on a page (see Figure 4.29).

Now let's take the same two lines and have them describe a series of curves. They now feel more flexible than formerly, but it's still not really possible to determine whether they represent a rounded three-dimensional or a graphic two-dimensional image. They may indicate a living creature or a river. Adding a bit of detail and depth to the sketch turns it into an earthworm (see Figure 4.30).

Squash and stretch and more squash and stretch

The quadruped vertebrates analysed earlier in this chapter contain bony 'hard' and fleshy or furry 'soft' forms that show contrasting forces when the animal moves. But how do you indicate forces affecting the movements of an earthworm body that is composed entirely of boneless curves?

The key to animating crawling animals is to view them as animated lines of action. This reduces animation to an absolute minimum: the line of action must convey the performance without the addition of secondary or overlapping actions. Parts of the worm or snake's body will appear tenser than others depending on the interplay between curved and straight sections in the animation. This tension is beautifully portrayed by T. S. Sullivant's illustration (see Figure 4.32) as the snake's body also suggests a coiled spring.

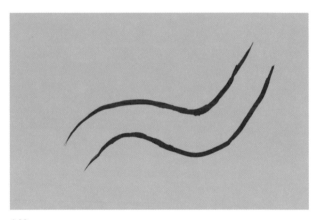

4.29
Two parallel lines

4.30
Added detail
A bit of added detail creates a simple worm character.

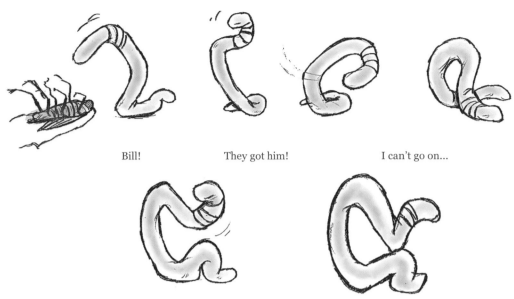

Bill!   They got him!   I can't go on...

And yet...   I have to consider the others.

4.31

Small creatures with big emotions
The strength of an animated character's pose does not depend on muscular strength. An animated worm's performance can show the same *emotional* force as that of a human being or vertebrate animal. This is the magic of animation. The strength of the performance does not depend on the size of the character. Small creatures can portray big emotions.

4.32

Eve and the Snake by T. S. Sullivant (1921)
The snake's body is tense in some areas and relaxed in others. The coil suggests that the snake could 'spring' into animated action.

4.33

The worm turns
Let us try portraying some emotions with the earthworm's body. In this illustration Pose 1 shows shock; Pose 2 shows happiness; Pose 3 shows anger and Pose 4 shows confusion. This simple character can assume different attitudes suggesting an entire body (as in Pose 1); or a portion of a body (a mouth is portrayed in Pose 2 and a fist in Pose 3); or it can incorporate graphic symbolism to describe an emotion, as shown in Pose 4.

5

Fantastic performance!

In the first section of this chapter you will learn how to create or re-create action for extinct and mythical animals where live-action reference does not exist. Examples and interviews describe how other animators handled these creatures while sometimes going against the accepted science of the time.

Monsters, both animal and human, are the subject of the second part of the chapter. These can be interpreted as pure aliens, split or dual human personalities that may transform into animals, and finally as monstrous or fantastic animal/human combinations. The final section describes the action and animation of weightless characters, using the movement of sea creatures as reference for animated acting in water and in outer space.

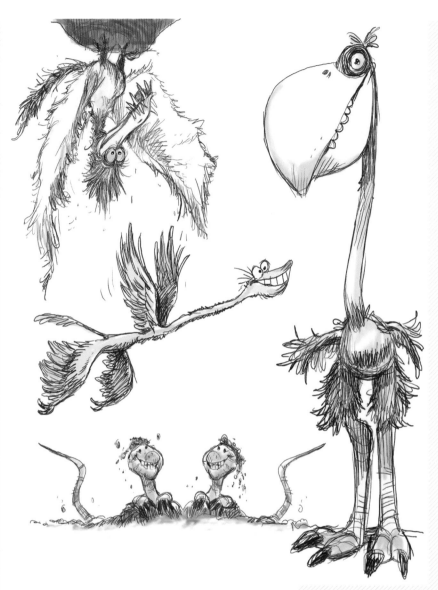

True dinosaurs can be stranger than fiction
In recent years furred and feathered fossils have been discovered;
one species that is now determined to have had four wings
was accurately animated by Winsor McCay in his 1914 film
Gertie the Dinosaur!

Natural inspirations for the supernatural

'The gift of fantasy has meant more to me than my talent for absorbing positive knowledge.'

– Albert Einstein, Swiss-American theoretical physicist, philosopher and author

Animation allows the film-maker to create beings that may inhabit a prehistoric Earth whose geography, gravity and ecosystems are very different from the one we know; or they may live in a fantasy world where earthly definitions and limitations of space, gravity, physics, logic, and anatomy need not apply.

The animation medium adapts well to both worlds. Let's first examine acting assignments for extinct Earth creatures that do not resemble living animals. Unless a comic effect is intended, as with Dino the Dinosaur in *The Flintstones* (1960–1966), the animators must research scientific theory to make their performance convincing.

Re-animating dinosaurs

How do you analyse the movement of a creature that no longer exists and whose anatomy differs dramatically from that of living species? The fact that birds descended from dinosaurs was recognised relatively recently; prior to this discovery animated dinosaur movement was usually based on scientific theories that were prevalent when the films were made. Dinosaurs were described as slow, cold-blooded animals during the 19th and most of the 20th century. Since animation must *move*, animators often took liberties with science so that the creatures could act as well as fight. Winsor McCay studied the movements of elephants while animating *Gertie the Dinosaur* in 1914 (correctly, according to modern theories of dinosaur movement) and created the first animated 'giant monster attacking a city' in *The Pet* (1918–1921).

Willis O'Brien animated dinosaurs using stop-motion puppets in *The Lost World* (1925) and *King Kong* (1933). O'Brien, a former palaeontologist and wrestler, used human wrestlers as reference for the battle between King Kong and a Tyrannosaurus Rex (see Figure 5.1).

O'Brien's Tyrannosaur moved rapidly, more like a modern mammal than the sluggish reptiles dinosaurs were assumed to be at the time the film was made. It walked upright in a 'tripod' pose, with the tail and legs providing support for the body. The tripod stance possibly made it easier for O'Brien to balance the puppets; he gave his tyrannosaur a flexible waist and neck to keep it mobile.

O'Brien based his dinosaur on the Tyrannosaur skeleton displayed in the American Museum of Natural History in New York City (see Figure 5.2). The skeleton went on display in 1915 in an upright striding position with its tail dragging on the ground, as was fitting for a gigantic lizard, and in accordance with scientific consensus. It would have been most disrespectful for anyone, *especially* someone who worked in a cartoon studio, to suggest that the skeleton's pose might not be correct. I had the good fortune to speak with Wolfgang (Woolie) Reitherman, the animator who discovered this.

5.1

Tripod stance
Willis O'Brien animated a Tyrannosaurus Rex fighting
with an upright 'tripod' stance in *King Kong* (1933).
Courtesy of RKO/The Kobal Collection

A tyrant lizard

Wolfgang Reitherman animated the Tyrannosaurus Rex for the 'Rites of Spring' sequence in *Fantasia* (1940). It was a brutal acting assignment in more ways than one. He could study the skeleton of the long-extinct creature but, since behaviour does not fossilise, there was no reference available at the time to indicate how a living tyrannosaur might have moved. The only film reference was Willis O'Brien's work on *King Kong*, which features both a tyrannosaur and a stegosaurus. But Woolie ran into a problem when he tried to draw and animate his tyrannosaur.

'*I couldn't get him to walk*,' Reitherman told me in 1982. 'We opened the sequence with a shot of the tyrannosaur standing upright in the same position as the American Museum of Natural History's mounted skeleton. The tail was dragging on the ground. It just *didn't work*. If he took one step while in that position, he'd have broken his back. I had to bend him over the centre of gravity at the hips to get him to move.'

As a matter of fact, Woolie kept the tyrannosaur moving in an upright attitude for most of the sequence, though the tail never dragged on the ground. The tyrannosaur is first revealed standing in the same pose as the museum's skeleton; there is a fast truck-in to its face. Every so often during the chase the tyrannosaur has to bend at the hip to snap its jaws at a smaller dinosaur, but each time it immediately stands up straight again. It is as if the animator was fighting his instinct to base the animal's stance on his knowledge of balance and movement, rather than what was commonly believed. Finally, during the battle between the tyrannosaur and the stegosaur, Woolie gives up on science and animates what he knows to be right. The tyrannosaur now holds its body at a 45-degree angle, its weight balanced over its centre of gravity at the hips.

In 1996, after a year-long restoration, the Museum of Natural History exhibited its tyrannosaur skeleton in a new, running pose. Its body was at a 45-degree angle and its tail was held high, counterbalancing the body, exactly as Reitherman animated it in *Fantasia*. Good animation and action analysis anticipated scientific theory by more than 50 years.

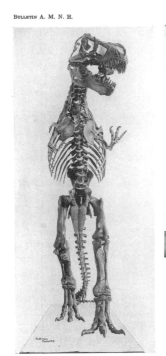

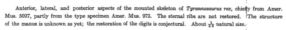

Anterior, lateral, and posterior aspects of the mounted skeleton of *Tyrannosaurus rex*, chiefly from Amer. Mus. 5027, partly from the type specimen Amer. Mus. 973. The sternal ribs are not restored. The structure of the manus is unknown as yet; the restoration of the digits is conjectural. About $\frac{1}{18}$ natural size.

5.2

A tyrannosaurus skeleton

The tyrannosaurus skeleton was originally mounted in a 'tripod' stance since dinosaurs were assumed to be cold-blooded lizards that used their tails for support.

Plate XXV from 'Henry Fairfield Osborn. 1917. Skeletal adaptations of Ornitholestes, Struthiomimus, Tyrannosaurus'. *Bulletin of the American Museum of Natural History* v. 35, article 43. Courtesy of the American Museum of Natural History.

5.3

A well-balanced pose

Wolfgang Reitherman's 1940 *Fantasia* animation (above left) anticipated the pose of modern tyrannosaurus skeleton mounts (above right).

Fantasia still © Disney Enterprises, Inc.

Photo © J.M. Luijt, used by permission through Creative Commons Attribution-ShareAlike 2.5 (Netherlands)

Fun with fossils

More recent dinosaur animation from *Jurassic Park* (1993) to *Ice Age: Dawn of the Dinosaurs* (2009) uses more modern interpretations of dinosaur stance and behaviour as animation guides. Curiously enough, dinosaur evolution takes odder and odder turns each time new fossils are found. Some, such as pterosaurs, are now revealed to have had feathers; other creatures, when reconstructed, resemble characters from children's books illustrated by Dr Seuss. A 'four-winged' dinosaur has been found – very similar to one animated by Winsor McCay in *Gertie the Dinosaur* – and also an alarming cross between a bird and a battleaxe that was dubbed the 'Demon Duck of Doom' by its discoverers. Scientists can now estimate how quickly some dinosaurs moved by analysing fossil footprint tracks. (None have ever been found with a groove in the middle that would indicate the track of a dragging tail.) Colonies of nesting dinosaurs have been unearthed in Canada and Mongolia and fossils of burrowing dinosaurs were discovered in Australia in 2009. Animators can find wonderful material and vary their performance of prehistoric creatures by reviewing scientific publications and adapting the most recent findings to the movement of their latest monsters.

5.4

Paleontological discoveries
Recent paleontological discoveries include feathered pterosaurs, four-winged and burrowing dinosaurs, and the 'Demon Duck of Doom'. New species are discovered every year, providing excellent research material for animators. A four-winged dinosaur appeared in Winsor McCay's *Gertie The Dinosaur* in 1914!

EXERCISE

5.1 Dinosaur research and animation

Visit your local museum of natural history. You may use scientific publications such as the **New Scientist** magazine or websites such as Sauropod Vertebra Picture of the Week <http://svpow.wordpress.com> as reference if you are unable to get to a museum to view actual fossils. **Do not reference motion pictures or television shows that recreate dinosaur action.**

- Draw several views of one mounted dinosaur skeleton. The animal should be a less-familiar one that has not appeared in many films; do not use tyrannosaurs, velociraptors, apatosaurus (formerly known as 'brontosaurus'), triceratops, pterodactyls or stegosaurs.
- Now draw sketches reconstructing how the creature might have looked in life. Many dinosaur skeletons were distorted and flattened during the fossilisation process; use your knowledge of anatomy to determine the original appearance of crushed or missing bones. Add muscles and body mass, then skin, feathers or scales if the specimen shows them. Use your imagination to indicate the creature's eyes, beak (if present), crest, or horns.
- Scientific publications now describe fossilised behaviour such as burrowing, running (from fossil footprint tracks), flying, nesting and herding. Analyse how your dinosaur may have moved by reviewing its skeletal structure. Your animated character might differ from the scientific interpretation – don't worry if this happens.
- Now set your dinosaur in motion. It may move any way that you wish, but strive for a believable quality. You may use living animals for reference at this stage. Estimate how much the dinosaur weighs, then thumbnail the creature walking, running, flying (if applicable), and interacting with a prop. Does it have a ferocious or docile disposition? For a comic touch, you could illustrate how a scientist might measure, test and possibly annoy a living specimen.

Natural inspirations for the supernatural

Modern monsters

Actors in suits, such as the one playing Godzilla in *Godzilla vs Hedorah* (1971) below, are often unsuccessful at creating an atmosphere of menace because the human's anatomical construction is visible in the scene.

Some monsters, such as Gollum in *The Lord of the Rings* (2001) and Dr Frankenstein's 'monster', were degraded caricatures of human beings and were most effective when performed by live actors, but I have personally rarely found aliens, dinosaurs, or non-human monsters convincing or frightening if they had human proportions.

Artistic interpretation allows you to modify human anatomy so that it is barely recognisable (as seen in the work of H. R. Giger opposite) which can produce more disturbing effects on the (human) viewer than a totally alien character.

5.5

Visible human anatomy
The human actor's anatomy is visible in the Godzilla suit and destroys the illusion of a giant monster on the attack.
Toho/A.I.P./The Kobal Collection

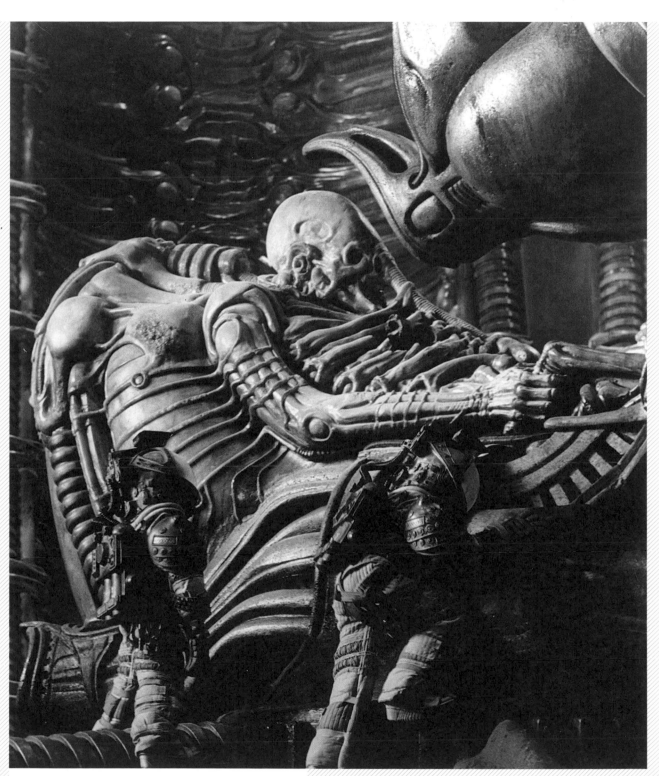

5.6

Alien

The creatures and settings of *Alien* (1979) were based
on the work of surrealist illustrator H. R. Giger.

Alien © 1979 20th Century Fox and The Kobal Collection

Hits and myths:
Animated characters based on cultural legends

Many cultures describe mythological creatures that share the Earth with humanity, and animators have often brought these beings to life. In fact, animation is the only way you could plausibly portray a creature as illogical as a centaur, which consists of the upper half of a man that is joined at the pelvis with the shoulders of a horse. In the real world, this would lead to anatomical redundancies and no end of embarrassment. The centaur has two ribcages, two shoulder girdles, and two pelvises, but only one pair of buttocks. The creature would have a hard time surviving in actuality (how would the 'horse' lungs breathe?) but it is believable in a fantastic context. Even though the centaur is a creature of fantasy it is still grounded in Earthly reality. In Figure 5.8 the same line of action carries through both halves of the centaur, unifying the design. The two halves of this centaur would move in the manner of each species, with the lower body using a horse's gaits and the upper half those of a human being.

Ray Harryhausen's Medusa from *Clash of the Titans* (1981) in Figure 5.7 blends elements of human and snake throughout the design and animation rather than grafting halves of two different species together. But it is her performance, based wholly on the animator's imagination, which really brings her to life. Medusa, whose body is more snake than human, is first seen crawling into her underground lair on her belly and then raising the human torso off the ground on its arms. She stands in the attitude of a striking cobra while destroying mortal men with her arrows and her lethal gaze.

Medusa's eyes are cold and unfocused and her acting is underplayed. She draws, nocks, and shoots arrows with near-mechanical precision. There is no reaction when one of her arrows hits a mark. Even though an aura of menace surrounds her, we sense no intelligence or motivation behind Medusa's movements. Medusa's soul has also merged with that of the snake and she lives only to bring death and destruction to others.

5.7

Medusa
Ray Harryhausen's Medusa in *Clash of the Titans* blended human anatomy and movement with that of a snake.
Courtesy of MGM/The Kobal Collection

5.8

A classic centaur
A representation of a classic centaur with the upper half of a human torso grafted onto the shoulders of a horse. The two halves will move differently when animated.
Illustration © 2008 by Adriana Pucciano

Legendary improvements: Animating the story

Medusa's bow and arrows are an addition to the original myth, which merely had anyone who viewed her face turn instantly to stone. The animation medium requires that characters move and interact with one another. The snake/human body does not move quickly, and Medusa's victims do not move at all. The legend need only describe a fantastic situation; the animated film must show it.

Certain illogicalities in this story became evident when it was translated from print to a visual medium. Why couldn't Perseus and his colleagues shield their eyes from Medusa and avoid her gaze? They could run faster than she could crawl. Medusa is also not aggressive in the original legend – she is asleep. Perseus simply looks at her reflection in a shield for surer aim and strikes off the sleeping monster's head. There is no struggle. The film-makers needed to have Medusa play an active role and threaten all the Greeks, not just Perseus, so as to maintain suspense in the sequence.

A bow and a quiver of arrows provided splendid opportunities for animation, made Medusa a menace even at a distance, and let her assume the lead role in her scenes. While the Greeks can attempt to hide from her gaze, the arrows are not so easily avoided. (Her gaze, though lethal, is a passive threat – the arrows are an active one.) Perseus uses *his own* reflection in a dropped shield to lure Medusa toward his hiding place and misdirect her gaze. He strikes her as she glides by, viewing her reflection only as he gingerly picks up the severed head. This is far more suspenseful than the original story and makes great cinema. Suitable props add acting depth to scenes of horror as well as comedy.

Medusa is an outstanding piece of animated acting. Ray Harryhausen's imaginative animation in this film, and many others, projects a totally alien quality that keeps his performances memorable and terrifying even in the age of computer-generated imagery.

A more recent human/animal blend turned actor Bill Nighy into an octopoid Captain Davy Jones with a crew of half-human, half-marine monsters in *Pirates of the Caribbean: At World's End* (2007). A CGI-animated cephalopod/human face was composited with Nighy's after the live-action performance was shot. The animators then based their 'creature acting' on Nighy's, integrating two performances within a single character.

5.9

Two performances in one
Bill Nighy as Davy Jones in *Pirates of the Caribbean: At World's End* (2007) was two performances in one: live-action blended with character animation.
© Disney Enterprises, Inc./The Kobal Collection

5.2 Fantastic human/animal design combination

Create your own fantasy human-animal hybrid. Please do not design pre-existing mythological creatures such as mermaids, centaurs, griffins, unicorns, harpies, or Minotaurs, and do not simply attach an animal head and tail to a human body.

➤ Blend elements of each species' design throughout the drawing. You may use more than one animal for this exercise.

➤ Try using non-Classical myths for reference. Many cultures have tales of hybrid creatures. They are usually malevolent but yours doesn't have to be. You may wish to describe the creature's characteristics in writing while drawing your designs.

➤ Draw thumbnails of the creature interacting with a prop in a positive and negative way. Consider its emotional state as well as the physical; does it have human or animal reactions, or a mixture of both? You may want to indicate the percentage in writing on the thumbnail sheet since this will influence your performance.

This exercise differs from Exercise 4.4 (human/animal combination) since there should be a fantastic aspect to the creature; its movement does not need to be based on reality.

Next >

In the next section we will see another way to have two bodies literally occupy the same space.

Dual natures:
Human/animal combinations

'One thing vampire children have to be taught early on is –
don't run with wooden stakes.'

– Jack Handey, American comic writer, comedian and actor

The transformer

Human beings that turn into other creatures are a staple of literature, superstition, and motion pictures. Some human characters turn into new incarnations of themselves. Dr Jekyll uses drugs to liberate part of his own personality as Edward Hyde, a being that usurps their shared body and embodies only the evil side of Jekyll's nature with no trace of the latter's goodness. Jekyll's external appearance is completely different from that of Hyde but that difference does not extend to the spirit. The 'normal' Jekyll remains a mixture of good and evil; Hyde's desires are always present in Jekyll's soul, and evil triumphs at the end of the story.

The animation medium is admirably well-suited to show the metamorphosis of a character's appearance and personality. In this section we will investigate various ways animators might accomplish this.

Jekyll and his dark twin Hyde are two aspects of the same man. Other fantastic creatures such as vampires and werewolves frequently maintain completely separate identities in transformed bodies. Dracula is a lifeless corpse by day and may retain the shape of a human or turn into a bat or a white mist at night. The werewolf of legend may appear fully human during the day but assume the shape of a wolf at night when the full moon rises, regaining its human form at daybreak. The division between two identities is not always complete; there are occasionally hints of the animal in the human incarnation's appearance and movement, as shown in this excerpt from the 1909 short story *Gabriel-Ernest* by H. H. Munro (also known as 'Saki'):

'The boy turned like a flash, plunged into the pool, and in a moment had flung his wet and glistening body half-way up the bank where Van Cheele was standing. In an otter the movement would not have been remarkable; in a boy Van Cheele found it sufficiently startling. His foot slipped as he made an involuntarily backward movement, and he found himself almost prostrate on the slippery weed-grown bank, with those tigerish yellow eyes not very far from his own. Almost instinctively he half raised his hand to his throat. The boy laughed again, a laugh in which the snarl had nearly driven out the chuckle, and then, with another of his astonishing lightning movements, plunged out of view into a yielding tangle of weed and fern.

"What an extraordinary wild animal!" said Van Cheele as he picked himself up. And then he recalled Cunningham's remark, "There is a wild beast in your woods."'

– Extract from *Gabriel-Ernest* (1909) by H. H. Munro ('Saki').

The boy's movements, which are clearly those of an animal, would be difficult for a live actor to reproduce but could easily be accomplished in animation. Saki never describes the transformation scene in his story but leaves it to his readers' imaginations. Motion pictures, and particularly animated films, must show this action onscreen.

5.10

Dr Jekyll and Mr Hyde
Dr Jekyll and Mr Hyde are not really separate individuals. There is always a trace of Hyde in Jekyll's personality.

Blocking and timing animated transformations

The speed and acting of the character's transformation from one body to another will vary depending on the effect that the animator wishes to produce in the audience. In Adriana Pucciano's illustration (see Figure 5.11) the transformation from man to werewolf plays as comedy because of the unexpectedness and rapidity of the change, which surprises the werewolf as much as his girlfriend. The acting on the two characters and the special effect are deliberately underplayed; the werewolf's body attitude remains the same after the transformation, indicating that it was instantaneous. Even though the werewolf is the lead character, the girl reacts to the change before he does.

A contrasting effect is created by having the transformation take place during a primary action. In Simon Ward-Horner's illustration (see Figure 5.12) the primary action is a run and a leap; the transformation becomes secondary action. The girl begins to change into a fox in mid-air and completes the transformation as she hits the ground. There are two poses where the girl's body is shown metamorphosing into that of the animal. The change begins gradually on one leg and then rapidly accelerates. The fox body will not 'pop' on screen since this action appears to happen very quickly; the intermediate drawings might not register on the viewer's eye since the entire animated action might take only two or three seconds of screen time. An excellent touch has the girl's *hair* metamorphosing into the fox's *tail*. Similar shapes merge easily in animation and artistic cheats are frequently used; silhouette, movement and the line of action are more important than literally transforming each part of the human anatomy into its animal equivalent.

A *morph* has the outlines of one body gradually shift to form the shape of a new one. This kind of transformation is extremely effective in horror scenes that need time to build suspense. A good example is the aging of the evil portrait in Oscar Wilde's *The Picture of Dorian Gray* (1890).

5.11

Werewolf transformation
An instantaneous transformation can create
a comic impression.
Storyboards © 2008 by Adriana Pucciano

5.12

Lady into fox

A girl turns into a fox mid-leap. The metamorphosis is not instantaneous, but still happens fairly quickly.

Were-Girl Illustration © 2008 by Simon Ward-Horner

5.13

Morph

A morph animates all sections of the design at once, producing a gradual change that can be extremely effective in some contexts.

Dual natures: Human/animal combinations

Going to animated extremes

I animated a transformation scene for an unreleased short film that took the concept to a ridiculous extreme. A witch has cast a spell upon herself that makes her beautiful for one night; she will resume her normal shape at sunrise. Since she is a very stupid witch, her idea of 'beauty' is open to dispute but her 'ugly' side is indisputable. The story point has a troll kiss the witch just as the sun rises, so that the spell wears off during the kiss. The transformation comes as a huge relief to the witch, but not to the troll. He runs off screaming in terror while the witch prances around delightedly shouting 'I'm myself again!'

The scene was so long that I thought it might be entertaining to lengthen the kiss and see the witch transform a bit at a time rather than all at once. I could animate one part of the 'pretty' design and turn it 'ugly', giving the audience a chance to see each change before advancing to the next part. The troll has his eyes shut while he is kissing the witch and doesn't see what is going on until her nose (the last part to change back), literally punches him in the face. It made for a very entertaining piece of animation.

How do you avoid making transformation scenes gimmicky and repetitive? Animators and film-makers develop new concepts by building on older ones. The key is to avoid literally repeating something that has gone before, and to always work your own variations on 'standard' action into the performance. This applies to all of your animation, not just transformation scenes.

5.14

A gradual transformation
These thumbnails show a witch's spell wearing off so that she turns back into her normal shape during a kiss. Visual puns abound in this scene; similar shapes in the two designs are animated at different speeds.

146   5. FANTASTIC PERFORMANCE!

< Natural inspirations for the supernatural · Dual natures: Human/animal combinations · Floating worlds: The weightless actor >

5.3 Animal into human transformation

Draw a series of thumbnails for a scene showing a human being turning into an animal, or an animal turning into a human.

➻ Start with the human and animal designs, then get a start and end pose for your transformation. Designs should be kept simple. Do not use bats, wolves or any other overused animal. Use an animal that is interesting and a bit of a challenge to you.

➻ You may want to set the action within a fairy tale or nursery rhyme to give this exercise a story context. Try using stories from different cultures. Do not imitate transformation scenes in existing animated films.

➻ Determine the range of motion of your characters. The animal's range will vary by species. Write down these qualities next to your 'start' and 'end' drawings.

➻ Next, plan your acting. What is the mood of the human? Of the animal? Is this transformation desirable, or is it a curse? Is it done at the will of someone else? Your acting will depend on the character's attitude toward this transformation. Write both characters' feelings next to your descriptions of their movement.

➻ Perhaps this transformation might be animated from the animal's point of view rather than the human's. Would this animal view the human body as a **monstrous** form?

➻ Once you have planned your scene, transform your character. Draw breakdown poses where necessary. You may wish to scan and time the sketches on a line tester.

➻ What type of transformation might work best? Is there more than one way to stage this exercise?

➻ How might an animal react emotionally if it suddenly turned into a human being?

Next >

Next, we will investigate how animated acting is influenced by its environment. You may find it difficult to act under water or in deep space, but this is not a problem for the animated actor.

Floating worlds: The weightless actor

'If there is magic on this planet, it is contained in water.'

– Loren Eiseley, American anthropologist and natural science writer

The Earth is a water planet. Seventy per cent of the planet's surface is covered by water; but scientists know less about the bottom of the Pacific than they do about the surface of the moon. It's a hostile environment for humans, but a great setting for animated characters to work in. The feature films *The Little Mermaid* (1989), *Help! I'm a Fish!* (2001), *Finding Nemo* (2003), *Shark Tale* (2004) and the television show *Spongebob Squarepants* (1999–present) are all set here. But they only scratch, or splash, the surface of possibility that this environment offers the animator. Animals that live in water have evolved the most varied anatomy, and the most varied methods of locomotion, on planet Earth. There is a gold mine of information here that can be adapted for animated characters whether or not they actually live in water.

Air's density is about one per cent that of water; dirt is more than twice as dense. Therefore, a creature, live or animated, that moves through water will meet much more resistance than they would if they moved through air and less resistance than the creatures that burrow through the earth. The aquatic environment will visibly affect water-dwelling characters at all times.

Comparative animation

Fish, and marine mammals such as whales and dolphins, all have highly streamlined bodies to help them move rapidly through water. The mammals' legs have evolved into fins or flippers since they never need to 'go ashore'. Some fish can actually fly short distances by rapidly propelling themselves with their tails and soaring on specially modified fins (see Figure 5.15).

Although the force of gravity does not have as strong an effect on them as it would on a land-dwelling creature, a feeling of weight and volume can be achieved by showing how the speed of a whale or dolphin's movements are affected by its size and the dense water that surrounds it. Sections of the body – notably tails, fins or flippers – provide motive power; these move faster than the animal's body and provide some contrast in animation.

Otters, sea lions, and seals live in both land and water. They swim effortlessly and can perform incredible acrobatics while doing so. Nature footage will provide valuable reference on how different sea and freshwater creatures travel on dry land (see Figures 5.18).

Other creatures besides fish and aquatic mammals also move on and through water. Here are a few methods used:

Paddling: Water birds have their feet modified so that they resemble oars. They coast on the surface of the water or dive to feed at the bottom. Water birds move in, or on, three elements: air, earth, and water. It's impressive to see a duck or goose running across the water when resuming flight (see Figure 5.17).

Flying: Penguins, whose waddling walk appears so clumsy and comical on land, 'fly' gracefully underwater using their wings (never the feet) for propulsion (see Figure 5.16).

A few movements are peculiar to only one or two species or classes of animals.

Hovering: Sea horses are the only fish with upright bodies. They propel themselves forward (and backward) with small fins that are on their backs, rather than at their sides.

Wriggling: Eels and some snakes can ripple their long bodies and swim at a good pace. Octopuses wriggle their arms and also use jet propulsion when necessary. Sea slugs and sea snails use a sort of rippling glide to move on the ocean bottom.

5.15

A flying fish uses its fins as wings as it propels itself into the air.

Photos by U.S. National Oceanic and Atmospheric Administration

5.16

Penguins 'fly' underwater.

Photo by Snowmanradio used under Creative Commons Attributions 2.0.

5.17

Water birds travel on, and under, the water's surface by paddling.

Photo by Nancy Beiman

5.18

Otters, sea lions, and seals use different forms of locomotion on land and in water.

River Otter photo by Tim Vickers. Sea Lion photo by Jarret Campbell used under Creative Commons Attributions 2.0.

Walking: Sea robins and some other fish can walk underwater on special elongated fins that function as 'legs'. Other fish such as mudskippers can actually do this on land, holding a mouthful of water and flapping along on their front flippers, pushing with their tails. Crabs walk or scuttle sideways on six legs (see Figure 5.20).

Armadillos can walk under water while holding their breath for nearly 20 minutes, which is the same amount of time that a whale can spend submerged. They also swim by paddling and propelling themselves by rotating their tails.

These animals, fish, and birds have made modifications to their anatomy or behaviour that help them navigate aquatic environments. Invertebrates are not restricted by internal skeletal structures, and some have evolved very creative ways of moving around in water:

Rowing: The water boatman, or backswimmer, is a small freshwater insect that swims upside down just underneath the water's surface. Its long rear legs resemble the paddles of a rowboat (see Figure 5.21).

Skating: Water-striding insects skate rapidly on top of the surface film of pond water. Humans can also skate on water when it has solidified into ice.

5.19

An interesting variation
Combine land and sea to produce interesting variations on animal locomotion.

5.20

Crabs walk, or scuttle, sideways on six legs and carry objects in their claws.

Photo by U.S. NOAA

5.21

Backswimmers and water boatmen move just under the surface of fresh water ponds.

Photo by Dietzel65 used under Creative Commons Attribution 2.0.

Miniature kingdoms

Other creatures travel by less classifiable methods. Microscopic creatures in a drop of water and the zooplankton in the ocean use cilia, pseudopods, and wave-like undulation to travel through the water. Entire ecosystems exist at different levels of the ocean.

When you start to move down deep into the ocean, the wildlife gets a lot wilder, and has even more unusual ways of getting around:

Jet propulsion: Squid, octopuses, and scallops send jets of water forward which propels them rapidly backward. The octopus and squid have a special chamber that they compress to jet the water outward; the scallop slams its shell halves together to rapidly jet away from danger. Jellyfish open and shut 'umbrellas' at the top of their bodies and are the only jet-propelled animals that move forward (see Figure 5.22).

Gonzo world

When you get into the ocean's abyssal zone, just about anything goes. Bizarre creatures, some smaller than a pea, use tiny flagellae (small whip-like structures with hair-like cilia attached) to propel themselves along. One particularly odd creature is shaped like a ball and swims by rotating like a slow and aimless top. There is even a creature that is, for obvious reasons, called the 'Dumbo' Octopus (see Figure 5.23).

Sometimes it isn't even necessary to descend into the abyss to find a creature using a new method of locomotion. In 2008, a creature that looked like a brightly coloured rubber beach ball was discovered *bouncing* along the ocean bottom right in the middle of a busy harbour. The creature, named 'H. Psychedelica' because of its vibrant colours and bizarre method of travelling, expels water from special chambers in its body for a jet-propelled assist while using its fins to push its body off the ocean bottom after each bounce. It also has eyes that face forward, like a human's (see Figure 5.24).

Scientists discover new sea creatures every year that are so completely surreal that it seems impossible for the animator to 'top' what nature has already done. But here, as in other instances, art comes not from copying nature but by combining elements of reality with those from your imagination.

Now that the zoology lesson is over, it is time to ask a few questions.

✎ Could a sea creature's movement be used for characters that work in other contexts?

✎ Might a being from deep space or another dimension have something in common with a creature from the ocean's abyss? (The monster in *Alien* was partially based on a chambered nautilus, which has a face that is as frightening as its shell is beautiful.)

✎ Could the movement of invertebrates be applied to larger, imaginary creatures with backbones, wings, or mammalian structure?

✎ Could an animated character 'swim' through another substance – fire, earth, or air as well as water?

Animation makes all of this possible.

5.22

Jellyfish use jet propulsion to travel.
Photo by U.S. NOAA.

5.23

No explanation is needed for the origin of the 'Dumbo' Octopus's name.
Photo by NASA.

5.24

Follow the bouncing fish!
(Yes, there is a real fish that does this.)
Illustration © 2009 by Elliot Cowan

Floating worlds: The weightless actor

A woman of the sea

Fantasy and legend created the mermaid, a creature that is half human and half fish. Irish, Scottish and Icelandic legend speak of the selkie, a girl who turns into a seal by putting on the animal's skin. One cartoonist drew an unhappy mer-person that had the fish half on the front end and human legs at the rear – but most representations of mermaids have human faces and fish tails. The mermaid's tail gives the animator many excellent opportunities for good design and strong lines of action in the key poses. Brittney Lee's design (see Figure 5.25) cleverly references Ray Harryhausen's Medusa animation by using a 'medusa anemone' for the mermaid's hair. (It also shows that the artist researched sea creatures when designing the character.) Clownfish live inside anemones, so the mermaid must also deal with her unwanted guests. This mermaid comes with her own built-in cast of secondary characters – in addition to the fish, smaller groups of anemone tentacles may move independently from her and from one another using their own lines of action.

5.25

Mermaid
A mermaid with swim-away hair and a slight infestation of clownfish.
Illustration © 2009 by Brittney Lee

Combination animation

Here is a simple exercise where the mermaid reacts to objects that she likes and dislikes (see Figure 5.26). Props and secondary characters give the mermaid something to work with. There is no need to add special effects like bubbles; the character poses create the impression of a watery environment.

Always start animating with simple shapes and action patterns, then gradually add more detailed movements – *never start with a complex character, or you'll never finish the scene.*

The mermaid's body action is blocked in first, the same way we animate a character on land, with one difference – the sea, rather than the ground, provides resistance and gives her movements a feeling of weight and solidity. Good construction, strong, clear poses, and variably timed secondary action on different parts of the figure also contribute to a feeling of weight in a 'floating character'.

These key poses are the bare bones of the scene. They only show the acting; they do not indicate timing. Secondary action on the mermaid's arms and tail appears when additional keys and breakdowns are added.

The mermaid's hair and fish are 'effects animation' that isn't necessarily influenced by the mermaid's movement, unlike 'normal' hair, which overlaps and follows the arc of a character's head movements whether it is under water or on dry land.

5.26

Mermaid props
The mermaid likes, and does not like, what she sees. Props provide her motivation. These main keys block the acting; additional keys and breakdown poses will vary timing for the body, hair, and tail and maintain the illusion of 'floating in water'.
Illustrations © 2009 by Brittney Lee

5.27

The mermaid's body will be animated before the effects on hair, fish, and tail are added.

Illustrations © 2009 by Brittney Lee

Straight shooting

This mermaid will be animated with a combination of two animation styles. *Keys and breakdowns* will first be set for the body, arms, head, and tail only, and then the inbetweens will be added.

After the main actions have been completed the anemone and fish effects will be added using the 'straight-ahead' animation method where Pose 1 is set on Frame 1, then Pose 2 on Frame 2, and so on until the end of the scene. The filmy fin on her tail may also be handled in straight-ahead animation at this time. This makes it easier for you to animate the undulating, curling tendrils of the anemone and darting movements of the fish.

If keys are set for these erratically moving elements at the same time as the mermaid's body and then inbetweened, the action won't work as well. It will most likely have to be reanimated and will take much more time to finish. Don't try to do everything at once. It's really more effective to do it this way.

It is possible for this mermaid to be upstaged by her own hair and the small fish if the audience's eye is misdirected. Unless the story calls for it, *hair, fins, fish, and bubbles are animated only after the primary and secondary actions and acting for the mermaid's head, body, arms and tail.*

Draw thumbnails of the simple character below, drawn by Elliot Cowan, moving under water. You may choose to have it paddle, dive, fly, hover, undulate, rotate, bounce or use jet propulsion. **Please do not use a 'walk' for this exercise unless it is a 'sideways crab-walk'. No human movement is allowed.** You may rework this design if you need to (lengthen flippers, and so on.)

➡ Work out thumbnails for its base (neutral) motion first. Can secondary action on fins, flippers, or tails help indicate that the character is moving through water?

➡ After you have created the basic movement for the creature, add an emotional context to the scene. Thumbnail the same action, this time with the creature moving as if it felt sad and lonely. Will this emotional input affect the poses, the timing, or both?

➡ Lastly, thumbnail the creature in the same action, this time with a happy and friendly attitude. You may use a prop to provide character motivation for both 'emotions' of the exercise.

The medium is the message

Now that you have completed the exercise, consider how this animation might work in other contexts. What if the creature was moving through fire, earth, or outer space rather than water? Would you need to make any changes to the action to make this animation work in the new environment?

What might happen if you took the creature movement from the previous exercise and used it for a human character? (Use the Sam design or a simple humanoid design of your own.) Thumbnail how the human form might incorporate the sea creature's action. The results may be surprising.

You might want to go back and redo exercises 5.2 on page 141 and 5.3 on page 147, this time incorporating the movement and body attitudes of one or more sea creatures. Which version is more effective or unusual?

Alternative mermaids

Next, design and animate a mermaid that combines a human and an aquatic creature that is **not** a fish. (Ursula, the half-octopus villainess in The Little Mermaid, is a good example of an alternative mermaid design.)

➡ Research the different creatures described in this chapter or find your own. Combine one with a human to design your own simple mer-person.

➡ Draw two or three thumbnails first showing how your mer-person likes, then dislikes, an introduced object or character. The two emotions may be conveyed in one set of thumbnails.

➡ Use the mer-person's entire body to show the emotions and have the action take place on or underwater.

➡ Do not add bubbles or effects. Your action should 'read' without them.

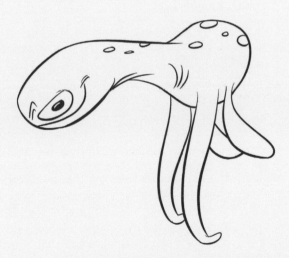

Next >

We will now see how character acting is affected by the *materials* at hand.

6

The performer as object

In this chapter inanimate objects come to life. We start with small household and office items and progress to entire houses, which may be characters in themselves or caricatures of human types. Trees and living wood will animate differently from furniture; you will see how period furniture design provides a context for animated acting.

Fabric is analysed in the second section. You will learn how to indicate weight in animated cloth and create the feel of different fabrics in motion. The third section investigates the properties of characters that are made of cloth, including rag dolls, scarecrows and clothing that has a life of its own.

Different materials

The materials that the character is made of will influence its movement. Fabric, straw, and paper do not squash and stretch the way flesh and bone do.

Moving the furniture: Bringing inanimate objects to life

'Come, let us all turn into pumpkins and roll upstairs into that old ballroom and see what ghosts are there! All right, let's not!'

– *If These Old Walls Could Talk* by Robert Benchley (1931)

Animation is literally defined as 'the art, process, or result of imparting life', and the medium is ideal for creating characters from objects that normally would not move and think for themselves. The Max Fleischer Studio excelled at bringing literally *everything* in their 'Out of the Inkwell' series to life in a cartoon universe where the city of New York and everything and everyone in it could become characters in the film. In *Ha! Ha! Ha!* (1934) a dentist's pliers has a dogfight with a pair of dentures; then a typewriter, two old cars, the New York skyline, and even tombstones burst into hysterical laughter when affected by 'laughing gas'. This animation is pure cartoon and owes nothing to live action. Visual puns abound. A typewriter turns into a giant grinning mouth as its keys morph into human teeth. There is the suggestion of a human face in the junked cars' grilles, bumpers and headlights. Gravestones 'slap their knees' while laughing. The only touch of realism in the animation is the use of cut-out photographs for the objects and backgrounds which, combined with distorted cartoon mouths, make *Ha! Ha! Ha!* even more bizarre than the typical Fleischer cartoon (if any of their films from this period could be described as 'typical').

6.1

Performing props
Animated cartoons can bring backgrounds and props to life along with the cartoon leads. A cartoon universe need not resemble reality.

Cartoon cartilage

The Fleischer 'animate-inanimate' characters
rarely moved in a way that suggested the
materials they were made of. Most were animated
in the 'rubber-hose' style. The handles of the
pliers in *Ha! Ha! Ha!* do not move up and down
while the jaws open and shut but form a 'body'
that slithers and bends and occasionally suggests
the movement of legs and knees. It resembles
a snake or reptile more than an object made
of hard metal. The dentures 'feel' more like an
inorganic substance since they maintain their
integral shape during the battle with the pliers.
Both participants lose their 'life' when the pliers
eventually manage to extract a tooth from the
dentures. Most characters in a Fleischer cartoon
appeared to be composed entirely of 'cartoon
cartilage' (see Ellen Woodbury's definition of this
substance on page 112).

In Disney's *Thru the Mirror* (1936), a mouse-sized
Mickey Mouse dances with human-scale animated
gloves and feuds with live cards that 'feel' like
they are composed of cardboard. In *Beauty and
the Beast* (1991), all of Beast's servants have
been transformed into household objects that
suggest the silhouette of their original human
bodies. When the servants resume their true
forms at the end of the film, the candlestick/man
is tall and thin; the clock/man is round faced and
heavyset, and so on. Human facial features are
retained, even on a candlestick. The appliances in
The Brave Little Toaster (1987) also incorporated
human faces into their design.

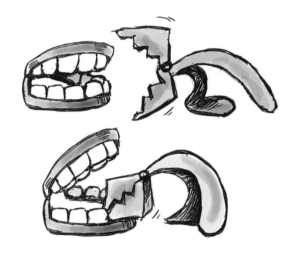

6.2

Rubbery objects
Inanimate objects in 1930s cartoons tended to have a 'rubbery'
feeling when brought to life.

Glazed expressions

Generally speaking, animation of ceramic, metal or wood will not deform as strongly as animated characters based on living creatures. In Jiin Park's story sketches an evil vending machine (see Figure 6.3) develops a 'face' and reacts to its impending doom with surprise and alarm.

Mrs Potts and her son Chip in *Beauty and the Beast* had human faces that took up most of their teapot-and-cup 'bodies', but the sugar bowl on Merlin's table in *The Sword in the Stone* (1963) used its lid to suggest both a rakishly tilted hat and a mouth, often at the same time, and its handles became flexible arms. Though it was ceramic it moved with a great deal of squash and stretch. This worked within the film's medieval context since the magical bowl was, after all, in a wizard's house.

Human emotions can be conveyed by characters that do not resemble humans at all. The computer-animated lamps in the 1986 Pixar short film *Luxo Jr.* portrayed a relationship between parent and child with body attitudes and movement since they lacked facial expressions or hands. The two robot leads in *WALL·E* (2008) used their mechanical and digital eyes for facial expressions and acting; only one of them had 'hands' and neither character had a mouth. Design restrictions, or limitations, can lead to inventive animated acting.

Tree of life

Trees and other vegetation will have varying textures in animation. Leaves may 'feel' like cloth, while a wooden trunk may not be very flexible (though it should move, if only slightly, when the rest of the tree is animated to give the feeling of 'life'). It is a good idea to block in the main action on the main trunk or stem first, leaving the crown a graphic shape. Then determine which part of the tree 'leads' along with the texture of its movement (an unbending oak will react differently from a flexible reed) and animate leaf movement as secondary action. The thickness of branches and foliage will vary the overlapping action.

I once had a student ask me how characters made of fruit might express emotions and perform as animated actors if they were hanging on a tree. I suggested that two leaves at the top of the fruit might function as 'hands' and 'eyebrows' as needed. Though the fruit could not move from its place, the camera *could*. Good staging and editing can create the illusion of character movement. Well-designed bunches of leaves might provide visual punctuation to set character moods, as shown in Figure 6.4. Experiment with other parts of the plant – possibly roots could be used as limbs, in addition to leaves, for a bit of variety.

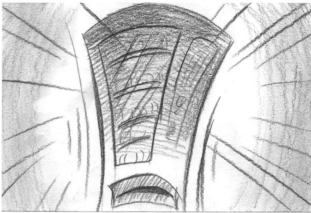

6.3

A vending machine with feelings

This vending machine suggests a human face. Some parts can be elastic and still maintain the 'feel' of metal.

Story sketches © 2008 by Jiin Park

6.4

A 'lively' tree and fruity characters

Tree trunks can form 'bodies' with branches or roots for 'arms'; faces can be designed around tree burls and limbs. Fruit on the tree can use leaves for expressions and for 'arms'.

A wooden performance

Furniture is designed to accommodate human forms and can sometimes suggest human actions without modifications in their design, as seen in the hilarious stop-motion animation *Roof Sex* (2001) by 'PES'. <http://www.eatpes.com/roofsex.html>. The association between the chairs and the human body parts that normally occupy them has been beautifully conveyed through the animation. Try imagining this action being performed by tables rather than chairs. It simply won't work. People *can* sit on tables, but it's not the first visual association that comes to mind.

Wood is strong, yet flexible, and 'animated' furniture should 'give' or squash slightly to create the illusion of weight when it is moving. Be careful, though. Evenly applied squash and stretch will make everything feel like a waterbed. Certain parts of the design (wooden legs or frames) might have stiffer movement than soft pillows or cushions on an upholstered sofa or chair. Everything depends on your medium, the design of your film, and the artistic philosophy of the animator.

Period pieces

Furniture styles have changed over the centuries and your animated characters might reflect their origins in their performance. For example, the Queen Anne chair was actually designed for that monarch and so might display a regal attitude (see Figure 6.6). A retro Eames chair might be a more sophisticated character than a plastic lawn chair. See if portions of the design suggest a human 'mouth' or 'eyes' to you.

Many years ago my family visited friends who had unfortunate taste in home decoration. They owned a dresser that resembled a grinning mouth full of teeth (I've never forgotten the horrible thing). A childhood memory can spark the creation of an animated character years after the original incident (see Figure 6.7).

6.5

Sentient seating
Sofa cushions can form a 'mouth' and pillows might resemble 'eyes'. Less flexible portions of the sofa can suggest the presence of a wooden frame. Bagpipes can suggest an octopus and a piano a ferocious alligator.

6.6

Period character
Acting styles can reflect furniture's country and period of origin, as with this Queen Anne chair.
Illustration © 2009 by Elliot Cowan

6.7

The Zombie Dresser
A horrible memory comes to life.

6.1 Bring life to an inanimate object that you see or use every day

Bring an everyday object to life. This can be an appliance, a utensil such as a fork or a knife, or a piece of furniture. Avoid using representational art, sculptures, or figurines of animals and people.

Please avoid using 'computers' for this exercise, especially the laptop or desktop screen. They have become animation clichés. Please also do not use 'cloth' at this time. **We'll get to that in the next section of this chapter!**

➤ Determine the emotional attitude of the character (object) before starting to thumbnail your scene. Does the tool/appliance/utensil like its job? Is it happy in its work? (I once designed a vacuum cleaner that hated its job since it had to eat dirt.)

➤ Draw thumbnails showing this object moving as if it were alive. You may suggest a resemblance to human features or actions.

➤ Have the object work with a simple prop to create a conflict. For example, a fork might try to pick up a piece of slippery spaghetti. You may add a second inanimate character if desired (a piece of toast might avoid an aggressive toaster). Do not use human or animal characters.

➤ What is the object made of? Is it flexible or hard plastic, metal or wood? Organic materials will animate differently from inorganic ones. Determine how much squash or stretch can be used on the character without sacrificing believability.

➤ Thumbnail one version where the object suggests some or all of its original materials' characteristics in the animation. Then try a second version of the same scene with the object handled in 'rubber-hose' style as in the Max Fleischer cartoons (see page 52). Which was more fun to draw, or watch?

Performing houses

A house's appearance can also suggest that of its human inhabitants. A very early cartoon (circa 1914) shows a husband imagining his house turning into his nasty mother-in-law's face (see Figure 6.8). Although the drawing is crude, the idea is excellent and reads well. Cartoonist James Thurber developed the theme in a similar cartoon a few decades later, with the gigantic woman's shape actually growing out of that of the house.

One of Winsor McCay's last films, *Dreams of the Rarebit Fiend: The Flying House* (1921) did not personify the house; it was strictly a prop. The Max Fleischer Studio frequently used animated buildings in their films, though usually only as incidental characters.

Disney's *The Little House* (1952) features a wonderful cast of machines and buildings. The title character's design suggests a woman's face. Backhoes and cranes resemble dinosaurs. Two Victorian brick buildings 'speak' through 'mouths' in their windows with the aid of waving shades and curtains. All of the buildings were viewed from the exterior. An animated house interior with furnishings, inhabitants, and textures was difficult and expensive to do before the advent of CGI. The house in Disney/Pixar's *Up* (2009) is viewed from inside, outside, and underneath. It becomes symbolic of the deceased wife by suggesting her spiritual presence rather than by developing a life of its own.

THIS IS HOW HIS COZY LITTLE MOUNTAIN BUNGALOW LOOKED TO HIM DURING THE VISIT OF HIS WIFE'S MOTHER

6.8

'This is how his cozy little mountain bungalow looked to him during the visit of his wife's mother'
A house becomes animated as windows and landscape turn into human features and clothing.

A house is not a home

Jamaal Bradley was a unit animator on the 'House' in the 2006 Sony Pictures Entertainment film *Monster House*, which was about a house that metamorphosed into a malevolent creature. Here he discusses some of the challenges posed by the title character. (Note: A 'stagger' is uneven action that is achieved in drawn animation by exposing images out of order so that a character appears to shake or shudder. It is far more difficult to do this in CGI animation than in hand-drawn, as Jamaal explains here.)

Q: You were one of the animators of the 'House' in *Monster House*, a film that used motion capture for all the human characters. Were you given free rein to 'perform' this house from imagination, or did you use any live-action reference footage?

Jamaal Bradley: We had a small team of around six who animated the 'House'. Mike Kimmel led us. When we first discussed how the House would move, the idea was that since the House was very old, it would need to shake in some manner. Mike said that we should 'stagger' the motion as the House reacted to other characters and as it moved through its environment. There were some tests that were done in the beginning of the House transforming from normal to the monster. Within those transformations the House would 'stagger'. For those readers who are not familiar with 'staggering' motion within animation, you basically are taking the normal path of action and delaying the motion. By offsetting keys moving backwards then forwards again until you get to the final point of the action, you give the illusion of 'staggering'.

Now having this happen over the 40,000 controls of the House was a tedious but very rewarding task once we saw the end result. Within all the staggering we gave our own performances life by discussing with the director his vision within a particular shot. Shooting endless amounts of reference gave me a good (acting) range to choose from and also enabled me to have a good base to present before I began animating. In a sense we were given free rein in that we could explore our own acting choices through our personal reference.

Q: What inspired you in your performance of the House? Did the dialogue track help, or did you base the House on creatures in previous monster films? (Or did you base it on anyone you knew?)

Jamaal Bradley: My inspiration when I shot reference for *Monster House* came from personal experiences. *I started to draw a lot of humanoid creatures at first and then I morphed the expressions I was drawing into a house.* It was pretty easy to create that idea visually since a house is pretty much the same [pattern] as a human face.

[Based on staging in] the sketches, I set up my camera and got on my hands and knees to try and make the movements I saw fit for the House. Being that the House is based on a heavyset woman, I tried to implement some femininity. This was not really working because the anger and rigidity of the House screamed nothing but 'monster'. *I had to rely on facial expressions to show any bit of life behind the glass and shingles.*

I used sad personal experiences in my life that had happened during that year to draw from. Pushing the boards above the two front windows, scrunching the shutters, and overlapping the wood would prove to be the best way to make the House express her emotions.

– Interview with Nancy Beiman (2009) (Italics added by author.)

6.9

Monster House

The 'Monster House' suggested a distorted human face. Animator Jamaal Bradley based the acting in his scenes of the House on events from his own life. Although live-action reference of a human actor was filmed it was used largely for blocking timing. Thumbnails and more detailed character drawings provided guides for the staging, acting and animation that could only be suggested by the live-action footage.

© 2006 Columbia Pictures and The Kobal Collection

Next >

And now, as promised, we will investigate the changing patterns of *cloth* in animation.

Material girl:
Fabric and cloth characters

'While Dorothy was looking earnestly into the queer, painted face of the Scarecrow, she was surprised to see one of the eyes slowly wink at her. She thought she must have been mistaken at first, for none of the scarecrows in Kansas ever wink; but presently the figure nodded its way down from the fence and walked up to it, while Toto ran around the pole and barked.'

– *The Wonderful Wizard of Oz* by L. Frank Baum (1900)

Tailored performances:
Fabric weight and movement

Before we analyse the action of characters made of cloth, let us first consider the properties of different types of fabric. As with everything else in animation, it is the impression, or *'feel'* of the fabric, rather than absolute realism, that matters. Stop-motion puppet animators can work with actual fabric, and entire CGI programs and plug-ins are designed to render and animate cloth; but even in these instances a simplified handling of the material can be artistically superior to literal interpretations.

The weight of clothing can be indicated by the number of wrinkles that appear at stress points. These folds will be consistent when clothes are on hangers, or on a life-drawing model holding a pose. Generally, heavier fabric will have a few large wrinkles while light fabric will have many. A human body's elbows and shoulders cause the fabric on a jacket, shirt or cape to compress and fold while less stressed areas on the sleeve do not. But sleeve fabric may drape and develop folds originating at wrist and elbow. Trousers/ pants develop stress points at knees, ankles, and crotch, and wrinkles will radiate from their origin at these points. Stretchy fabric has fewer wrinkles.

A good life-drawing class will include costumed models that allow the students to observe the different ways fabric drapes on the human figure. You will also draw people's clothing in your sketchbook. It is important to always remember that there is a body beneath the clothes and block it in before drawing costume details, or else your sketches may become flat and two-dimensional.

Animators must convincingly show how cloth reacts to a body in motion, not one that remains in a consistent modelling pose. Clothing and fabric in animation are usually handled as secondary action reacting to a character's movements (although they may have a life of their own in animation, where anything is possible – we will return to the fantasy element later in this section).

The weight of clothing can also be indicated by its reaction to movement.

- Heavy fabric will react by moving a few frames after the primary action, unless the original action is very violent.

- Lightweight fabric responds quickly to even small actions, and the finest materials might be affected by the actions of air currents and wind as well, so that they drift or trail behind the wearer.

6.10

Dorothy and the scarecrow from
The Wonderful Wizard Of Oz
The description of the scarecrow 'nodding' his way down
from the fence will create a different picture of its loose,
floppy movement in each reader's mind. Baum doesn't
explain how the scarecrow moves with the pole stuck up his
back (Dorothy removes it after he arrives.) W. W. Denslow
avoids this problem by illustrating the stillness just before
the scarecrow comes to life, but animators must show all of
this action onscreen; it cannot be left entirely to the reader's
imagination.

Drawn by W. W. Denslow (1900)

6.11

Sketchbook observations
Wrinkles in clothing radiate from stress points caused by the
body wearing it. You can observe everyday costume details
in your sketchbook.

6.13

Thin fabric
Thin fabric may show numerous folds and be influenced
by air currents as well as by the wearer's movement.
Photos of dancer Loie Fuller (1902) from the Library of Congress

6.12

**Folds and wrinkles in clothing remain consistent
when a model holds a pose.**
Illustration © 2009 by Dean Yeagle

Fashion movements

In the 1911 illustration shown in Figure 6.14 the women are wearing the stiff corsets that were fashionable at the time, so the fabric on the upper portions of their dresses has no wrinkles. The woman at the left wears a 'harem skirt', which was considered shocking. The numerous wrinkles on her pantalettes tell us that they are made of very thin fabric. A tight overskirt in a heavier material limits her leg movements to an up-and-down 'trotting' walk, or she might glide along in the 'royal walk' discussed on page 74. Her hat feathers could move up and down during animation; her purse is already showing some of this overlapping action.

The illustration uses animation techniques to show character movement and the weight of different fabric. This is because:

- The weight of the fabric is shown by the movement of the cloth, not by the number of lines used to indicate wrinkles.

- The tails of the men's summer suit jackets and the skirt of the woman at the right appear to be lightweight fabric, billowing like sails as they move.

- Simple wrinkles appear at stress points on the back of the woman at the right, on Harem Skirt Lady's harem pants, and on the men's jackets.

- Smaller wrinkles at the men's elbows and knees are hinted at, not shown.

- Shading is used sparingly.

- The men and the woman at the right appear to be walking much faster than Harem Skirt Lady since their legs have a larger arc of movement.

- Harem Skirt Lady has the most detail since she is the centre of interest.

- It is far more effective to show the 'feel' of cloth by using artistic shorthand than by attempting to keep track of each line or fold in animation. Stop-motion and hand-drawn animation can do this if given the time. CGI animators would find wrinkled material a nightmare to create and work with.

Remember that animation is an artistic interpretation, not a literal recreation of live action. Believability is more important than realism.

Figure 6.15 shows two sets of thumbnails experimenting with how Harem Skirt Lady might animate. She trots or hops in the first test since the tight skirt makes her legs' arc of movement very small. Her corseted upper body will not distort much in animation. The volume and movement of her legs underneath the skirt must be considered if she is animated in 'caricatured reality' style. The second, more graphic, approach keeps the skirt a solid shape while her feet move rapidly and improbably below the hem like those of a scampering terrier. In both tests, there is a great deal of overlapping action on her purse and in the feathers on her hat.

There is no 'one' way to animate anything; experimentation is the soul of animation.

6.14

Differently timed walks
This illustration portrays differently timed walks on figures wearing a mixture of lightweight and heavy clothing. Fabric's weight and texture can be suggested by its reaction to a primary action (walking) rather than by internal folds or lines.

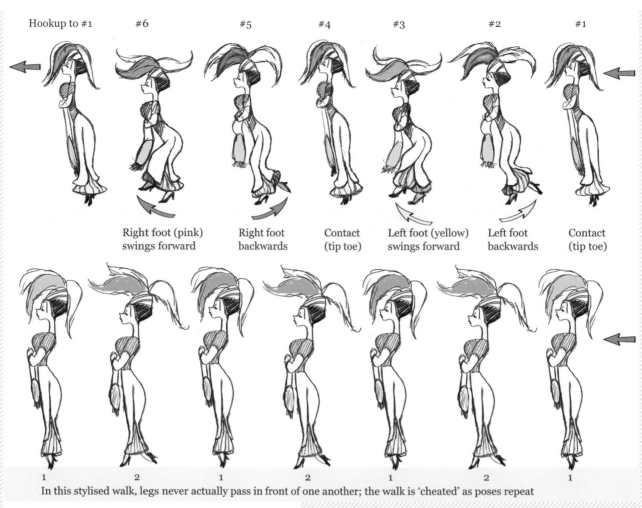

Hookup to #1   #6   #5   #4   #3   #2   #1

Right foot (pink) swings forward   Right foot backwards   Contact (tip toe)   Left foot (yellow) swings forward   Left foot backwards   Contact (tip toe)

1   2   1   2   1   2   1

In this stylised walk, legs never actually pass in front of one another; the walk is 'cheated' as poses repeat

6.15

Two ways of walking

One walk caricatures reality, the other goes for a purely graphic effect.

A rag and a bone and a hank of hair

A 'ghostly' character is sometimes portrayed as a semi-transparent, filmy, drifting being. It may not have legs or arms; its entire body could resemble cloth with no body underneath. The head might lead the action and pull the drifting body along almost as if moving through water. Effective ghosts might be animated using invertebrates (land or sea) as inspiration. Figure 6.16 shows a ghost with a jellyfish-like method of jet propulsion. Are there other creatures whose movements might suggest otherworldly or ghostly animated action to you?

One or two ripples may animate from one end of a fabric edge to the other to indicate stylised wrinkles, in a manner originally suggested to me by animator Tissa David, as illustrated in Figure 6.17. While Tissa's method was intended to portray the movement of ordinary fabric, an eerie effect could be created by having the ripples continue even when the ghost is not moving. A 'ghostly' or 'underwater' feeling can result if the rippling action animates independently from the figure's movement. This can help give an otherworldly feeling to the animation.

Alternatively the ghost's usual clothing may react differently from normal, as when Marley's Ghost appears accompanied by the breath of the Underworld in Charles Dickens' *A Christmas Carol.*

John Kendrick Bangs, in *The Water Ghost of Harrowby Hall* (1894), described the spirit of a drowned woman who appears as *wet* cloth. In this instance, the ghost's sodden robes could hang in heavy folds from stress points most likely at the shoulders, elbows, and wrists, and her hair would 'stream' across her shoulders. This ghost is part liquid – she 'ripples' in response to an order. The animation of fantasy creatures largely depends on the needs of the story.

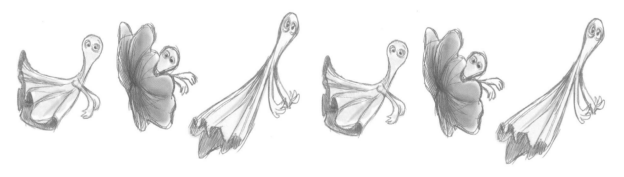

6.16

Ghostly movements
Animated ghosts may resemble 'bed sheets' or be composed of filmy, transparent fabric, which feels as if it is moving through *water* rather than air.

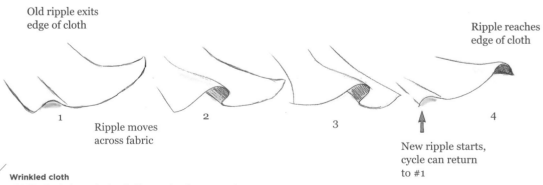

Old ripple exits
edge of cloth

Ripple reaches
edge of cloth

Ripple moves
across fabric

New ripple starts,
cycle can return
to #1

6.17

Wrinkled cloth
Wrinkles in cloth may be implied by moving them around the edge of the fabric in a 'wave' motion.

6.18

Jacob Marley and the Water Ghost
The ghost of Scrooge's old associate, Jacob Marley, is a transparent walking corpse whose 'upward' secondary action is created by a hot wind from the Underworld below. The Water Ghost of Harrowby Hall has her hair and clothing drawn downward by water.

The same face: the very same. Marley in his pigtail, usual waistcoat, tights and boots; the tassels on the latter bristling, like his pigtail, and his coat-skirts, and the hair upon his head.... Scrooge, observing him, and looking through his waistcoat, could see the two buttons on his coat behind.

– *A Christmas Carol* by Charles Dickens (1843)

The flour sack

Beginning animators will be familiar with the 'flour-sack exercise' in which a half-filled sack of meal is animated to illustrate the principles of squash and stretch on an animated body. Frank Thomas and Ollie Johnston showed in their seminal book *The Illusion of Life* (1981) how this simple shape can indicate a variety of emotions and attitudes without the use of facial expressions. The flour sack is only capable of performing full-body acting; the animator is forced to concentrate on primary action rather than secondary action (such as facial expression, movement of hair or clothing).

The flour sack is a stand-in for a human character or a cartoon animal, and its movements normally reflect this. It is not often treated as if it was really made of fabric with a texture and weight that might influence its action. Let us next consider what might happen if this were the case.

6.19

The flour-sack exercise
The flour-sack exercise is not concerned with maintaining the 'feel' of cloth; it teaches weight, volume and simple full-body acting.

Put a sock in it

I once drew storyboards at Gerhard Hahn Filmproduktion GmbH, a well-known Berlin animation studio, for a charming story about a lonely slipper named Schlupp. The poor slipper is first seen mourning the loss of his brother Schlapp, who one day went to the washing machine with a pair of socks and was never seen again. Schlupp is suddenly abducted from the shoe closet by a dog that runs out of the house and abandons the slipper in a gutter. There, Schlupp meets a delightful (and single!) lady's glove. Schlupp defends his new friend from a nasty rat by kicking it down a sewer. The lovers wind up as part of a modern artist's 'found-art' installation.

Inanimate characters can be extremely entertaining performers and take full advantage of the animation medium, as demonstrated in animator Carlo Vogele's *For Sock's Sake* (2008), which he created at the California Institute of the Arts by combining painted backgrounds with stop-motion animation. Here, Carlo comments on his inspiration and work methods:

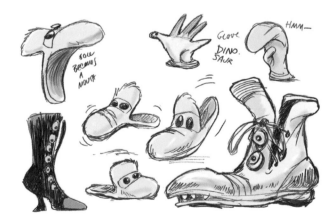

6.20

Acting shoes
Buttons and decorations can suggest eyes on a shoe; a glove can pantomime acting without additions.

6.21

For Sock's Sake
Carlo Vogele's *For Sock's Sake* suggests certain human 'types' entirely with a cast of clothing.
Illustrations © 2008 Carlo Vogele

'The idea for animating clothes came to me while playing around with my socks and pretending they were alive and could talk (the socks in the film are actually my own socks!)

'Ever wondered why there is always one sock of a pair that goes missing? Now you know!

'The biggest challenge was to animate the clothes in a smooth, fluid way. They would constantly wrinkle and fold in ways I didn't want them to.... I first used wire inside the clothes to control their motion, but it made the fabric look stiff and suggested that there was someone inside them, whereas I wanted to get the illusion that they were moving on their own, without any skeleton or armature inside. So after several tests I came up with the idea of small magnets that I placed inside the clothes, which I laid flat on a glass panel and placed other magnets underneath, so I could animate the clothes without touching them, frame by frame, with a downshooting digital still camera. It worked pretty well. But the hardest part was the blue jeans pants character, because they were so big!

'I guess the magic of this work lies in the fact that people relate instantly to the clothes characters. There is no taste difference whether you like or dislike the design, because they are just clothes, objects we all wear daily and are used to manipulate every day.

'There are a few clothes I wanted to include in the film, but had no time to: a pair of pink Hello Kitty slippers and a whole group of women's underwear gossiping in the bedroom....'

– Email to Nancy Beiman (2009)

For Sock's Sake can be viewed at <http://carlovogele.blogspot.com>.

The stamp of personality

Socks can suggest personality depending on their ornament and pattern, and by the way in which the owner's feet move. Foot movement, with or without a sock, can show:

✎ Anger (stamping)

✎ Shyness (scuffing, twisting foot, rotating on tiptoe)

✎ Decisiveness (marching, walking)

✎ Happiness (jumping)

There are many more. A sock's shape can also suggest a 'face' when it is turned upside down.

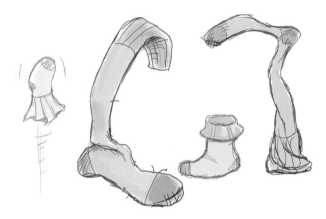

6.22

Expressive socks

An ordinary sock may suggest its human owner, or an animal, depending on how it moves.

TIP

Visual puns

The stop-motion films of 'PES' are excellent examples of *visual punning* where one object or action suggests another. PES uses ordinary found objects and textures in associations outside of their original context. *Western Spaghetti* (2008) creates the texture and movement of 'sauce' with animated cloth. *Western Spaghetti* may be viewed at <http://www.eatpes.com/western_spaghetti.html>.

Thumbnail a scene or short sequence featuring one adult and one child's sock illustrating this concept: **'Both socks need to clean up in a hurry.'**

First consider the materials the socks are made of; one of our actors will be a woollen knee-high sock, since that is a heavy fabric that won't wrinkle much. The other will be a child's small cotton sock. The large sock might move like a snake or worm but socks will distort and twist like cloth while a worm will 'feel' more like rubber. (Socks inflated like balloons and crawled like inchworms in the **'Caterpillar Room'** sequence of Jan Švankmajer's 1988 stop-motion feature <u>Alice</u>.)

Maybe the tiny child's sock has to hop rather than crawl. Or the socks might have the same 'walks' that their owners do, minus the volume of the human foot. The socks might even suggest the appearance and movement of animals. Many years ago I stitched two of mine together to form the upper and lower jaws of a donkey hand-puppet.

You will perform these characters without the use of eyes or faces, as we saw with the earthworms on page 126. It's easy to act out their timing with your hands.

Next consider the relationship between the characters. This will shape your animated performance.

➤ Are the characters related to one another? Since the adult and child socks are instantly identifiable (even the sex of the child, depending on colour) is it possible to suggest a parent-child relationship in your animation?

➤ What is their emotional state?

➤ Do they like one another?

➤ Are the socks representing human characters or animals, or just being themselves?

➤ Do they both want the same thing, or do they have opposing goals?

➤ Do they successfully complete this task?

(The acting will develop from their personalities and their relationship, which must be set first.)

Write your thoughts about how these fantasy creatures move before starting to draw thumbnails. Will they move 'sole down', 'sole up', or using a combination of both? Whatever their mental state, these socks should always 'feel' like cloth. Now block the action in thumbnail poses. You may wish to write the emotional state of each character on the same page as the sketches, particularly if attitudes change during the exercise.

Use the thumbnail methods mentioned in earlier chapters to help you set mood and character. Write notes on your drawings and don't be afraid to change them. You may think of more than one interpretation.

Rag time

A rag doll is made entirely of cloth. She will resemble a human being but since she has no skeleton to support her, she will be top-heavy and her limbs might buckle under the weight of the body. What sort of stuffing is inside the doll? These factors are as important to the performance as her emotional attitude.

In the confrontation shown in Figure 6.23, between a rag doll and a plastic fashion doll, a hard plastic arm detaches easily and is just as easily reattached, maintaining its shape all the while. The rag doll is loose, floppy and much more flexible than her adversary.

In Figure 6.24 the rag doll tears off her cloth arm to replace it with another one made of hard plastic. The storyboard does not indicate timing; if the fabric of the doll's body is fairly strong and the scene is sufficiently long, an animator might have the doll struggle a bit with the arm before it tears.

Animated rag dolls may vary spectacularly from one another since no two are alike.

- Rag dolls can move like flour sacks; but some dolls might have the flour settle more than others.

- Their faces and bodies could react the way clothing reacts on human beings. Perhaps their faces could develop folds and wrinkles to express emotion or show age.

- Stuffing can be lumpy and uneven, affecting movement.

- Arms and legs are boneless and highly flexible. There could be a lot of overlapping action in animation.

- The rag doll could move in an uncoordinated fashion, with different parts of the body leading at different times. Heads and arms can rotate 360 degrees if necessary.

6.23

Rag doll vs plastic doll
A plastic arm retains its shape when detached and
reattached in a battle between a plastic doll and a rag doll.
Story sketches © 2008 by Hyein Park

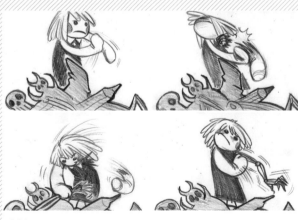

6.24

Switching arms
The rag doll uses a toy skeleton's arm to replace a cloth one.
Story sketches © 2008 by Hyein Park

6.25

Two very different rag dolls
No two rag dolls will be the same in appearance or
movement, and that is part of their charm. Stuffing may
settle, fabric will vary, and all of this will affect the animation.
Illustration © 2009 by Elliot Cowan

Cloth makes the man

Scarecrows share some of the same characteristics as rag dolls in animation but with one important difference: they have a rudimentary 'skeleton' of sticks that holds their arms out in an attitude that some people find unnerving. This skeleton can be dispensed with so that the scarecrow movement has a boneless quality. But since scarecrows are always stuffed with straw, they may still be less flexible than a rag doll.

The Scarecrow of Oz is frequently taken apart like an old suit, as described in the excerpt from *The Scarecrow of Oz*. Could the different parts of a scarecrow's body have a life of their own?

6.26

A stiff scarecrow
A scarecrow's stiff straw stuffing and wooden 'skeleton' makes its body less flexible than that of the rag doll.
Scarecrow © 2009 by Barbara Dale and Alan Grabelsky

Only a short time elapsed before a gray grasshopper with a wooden leg came hopping along and lit directly on the upturned face of the Scarecrow's head.

'Pardon me, but you are resting yourself upon my nose', remarked the Scarecrow.

'Oh! Are you alive?' asked the grasshopper.

'That is a question I have never been able to decide', said the Scarecrow's head. 'When my body is properly stuffed I have animation and can move around as well as any live person. The brains in the head you are now occupying as a throne are of very superior quality and do a lot of very clever thinking. But whether that is being alive, or not, I cannot prove to you; for one who lives is liable to death, while I am only liable to destruction.'

'Seems to me', said the grasshopper, rubbing his nose with his front legs, 'that in your case it doesn't matter – unless you're destroyed already.'

– *The Scarecrow of Oz*, L. Frank Baum (1915)

The objective of this exercise is to thumbnail and/or animate walk cycles and a short scene or sequence with a rag doll girl and a scarecrow man.

We will modify the 'Sam' character from Chapter 1 for this exercise. Sam the Rag Doll has her arms and legs tied off like salami to imitate the cloth body. There is no skeleton. Animate hair and clothing as simple shapes; do not worry about individual strands of 'yarn hair' for this exercise. Sam the Scarecrow appears to be made of clothing but also has a wooden 'skeleton' – and only in a few areas. It is essential to begin with simple shapes when animating complex characters that contain a variety of textures. This applies to clothing, mermaid's tails and our scarecrow and rag doll.

Rag doll is floppy and has no skeleton

Scarecrow has elbow and knee joints

6.27

Sam as a scarecrow and a rag doll
Use these modified 'Sam' designs for this exercise. The scarecrow has a simple wooden skeleton while the rag doll has none.

Wobbly walks

Thumbnail and animate a walk for the scarecrow and rag doll to see how their movements differ. (When getting acquainted with a new character, animators usually start with a walk cycle since it helps set the attitude and 'repeats', so that mistakes can be recognised easily.)

➤ Block in body action first. Leave clothing and hair for last.

➤ The scarecrow and rag doll may be top-heavy, and always on the verge of falling over. You must determine how coordinated they are.

➤ You will also determine their mood; are they happy, sad, tired, confident, or shy?

➤ Perhaps the scarecrow and rag doll walk with different 'leads'. You may wish to review 'The Ages of Man and Woman' in Chapter 3 for some suggestions.

➤ Their walks can resemble a 'drunk walk' – try blocking the body and head in first and adding arms and legs as secondary action, as shown in Figure 6.28.

➤ Overlap on hair and clothing is added last, possibly as straight-ahead animation.

➤ The rag doll should move in a way that suggests her femininity. Perhaps the 'female walk' Art Babbitt describes on page 72 can be caricatured here.

➤ A 'floppy' or soft feeling can result if 'moving holds' are used. Even when the bodies are still, an arm or leg or piece of clothing can still be in motion.

Draw body and limbs first, then add clothing and hair last

Moving hold at end keeps 'floppy' feel to the animation

Colouring in one arm and one leg prevents mixing up limbs during a spin in a rag doll dance

Scarecrow thumbnails are very rough. Wrinkles are implied in outline, not drawn in detail. His body movements are a bit less flexible than the rag doll's.

6.28

A lack of balance
A scarecrow or rag doll can be as unbalanced as a 'drunk'.
Masculine and feminine action will vary the performance.

Advanced exercise

Next, thumbnail a short scene or sequence for this scenario. (You may wish to return to this exercise after reading Chapter 7.)

'Scarecrow bows to Rag Doll. Rag Doll presents her hand for a kiss, and Scarecrow tries to kiss her on the mouth instead.'

Consider these points before you perform this scene:

➤ Does Rag Doll want Scarecrow to kiss her? Does she **like** him?

➤ Does Scarecrow actually kiss Rag Doll? Does he **like** her?

➤ Can Scarecrow bow gracefully? Does he have any problems doing this?

➤ How do both of them react if the kiss is/is not successful?

➤ Are there any props that might help show their relationship and help convey the emotional content of the scene? (It does not have to be comic.)

➤ Think of human types when animating these characters. Are they caricatures of reality? Do we feel sorry or happy for them?

➤ Reference: Nathaniel Hawthorne's bittersweet short story Feathertop: A Moralized Legend (1852), which can be read on the Internet, is about a scarecrow that a witch changes into a man. He falls in love with a human girl, only to lose all happiness when he sees his true appearance in a mirror. Stories can set moods and put you in the right frame of mind to perform serious emotion with fantastic characters.

Consider these additional points **after** you have completed the scene.

➤ Does one character appear to upstage the other? Which one do you want the audience to look at? Does the lead character change during the scene?

➤ Did the acting read as you intended it to?

➤ Was it more difficult to stage action on two characters?

Next >

We will next consider something that is *difficult* but not *impossible*... how to animate and perform several different characters in a scene simultaneously.

7

Double timing: Animating character interactions

Most animated films and scenes have characters working in groups. In this chapter you will learn how to determine the lead character in a scene and how to block the action so that secondary characters do not upstage the action or distract the viewer's eye from important elements in the scene. You will also learn how to shift character leads and perform several characters simultaneously while varying the acting and without showing your technique. The chapter starts with two characters, discusses the animation of larger groups in the second section and finishes with a rousing crowd scene.

Changing leads

Characters will 'change leads' in multiple-character scenes. The animator directs the viewer's eye to the most important character by varying movements and timing.

Staging and composition

'You can move some of the characters all of the time, and all of the characters some of the time, but you cannot move all of the characters all of the time.'

– Paraphrased from Abraham Lincoln (with apologies)

Animators' staging concerns are similar though not identical to those of illustrators. In both media the viewer's eye must 'enter' the frame and immediately be led to the focal point or character in the scene, then to the secondary characters and background details in the order that the artist intended. A cluttered design can interfere with the storytelling, as we see in the illustration of a couple in a greenhouse (Figure 7.1). The layout uses an X-shaped composition centring on the man's head, but we are distracted by the fussy detail in the background and on the woman's dress. It is difficult to tell where the characters end and the backgrounds begin. (This technique may sometimes be deliberately used for comic effect.)

In contrast, Phil May's 'Gutter-snipes' illustrations from 1896 (Figure 7.2) place the characters in specific locations and relationships with the action clearly staged. Our eye is directed to central figures (the dark-coated girl in the Hopscotch illustration; the tall girl leading the toddler in 'Little Mothers', and the boy holding the ball). The two children in the lower right-hand corner are staged in such a way that our eye is first drawn to the face of the small boy, then rightward to the girl. Western culture reads images and text from left to right; so even though the girl dominates the composition she is not the focal point of the scene.

In illustration, the drawing remains still while the eye 'moves' around the frame. The reverse is true in animation. Animators design artwork that moves through time and space. Frame compositions and character relationships are in a constant state of flux as the characters' position and volume change over time. Even the 'frame' of the image is not constant since the camera is also often in motion. The viewer has a set time (a scene or sequence) in which to view the performance. Individual animation frames or drawings are not an end in themselves, but the means to an end. Layout and staging will help direct the eye but poorly staged or blocked animation can negate designed contrasts in character and background, undermining the acting and storytelling.

7.1

A cluttered design

A cluttered design gives no direction to the viewer's eye.

Drawing by 'Sarfa' for *Judge* magazine (1914)

7.2

Gutter-snipes

Phil May's 'Gutter-snipes' includes several excellent examples
of group character composition.

The animated monologue

Animated characters do not often work alone. Chuck Jones' *Duck Amuck* (1953), produced by Warner Brothers, has a lonely Daffy Duck attempting to navigate a hostile cartoon universe while being tormented by an unseen assailant who is breaking all established rules of storytelling, composition, editing and character design consistency. Daffy does not perform in total isolation. For most of the picture he protests, pleads, and attempts to bargain with an offscreen 'Buster' who appears to be sitting in the audience. (This film must be seen theatrically to achieve the intended effect.) In one scene the projector image slips and Daffy has an argument with his double. The 'fourth wall' is broken so that Daffy's reactions to the film's wildly changing universe appear in context; his presence provides the film's only continuity.

Solo performances are rarely seen in longer productions since it can be difficult to maintain audience interest in the character and sustain the film's pacing. A lone character will only come to life if it is reacting to other elements and tensions in the story.

7.3

Commercial mascot
Solo characters are frequently used in commercial films.

Blocking the action: Follow the leader

Most animation assignments involve two or more characters working in the same scene with the animator timing and performing all characters simultaneously. This does not mean that the characters in a scene move all at once or that their actions are equally emphasised – quite the opposite!

One common mistake made by beginning animators is to have *all* of the characters moving *all* of the time. The main character may still be the focal point of the scene, but the other characters' action can be extremely distracting and the audience will not be sure where to look. The actors in the scene will compete with, rather than support one another.

Before beginning a scene with more than one character it is necessary to determine which one initiates the action and which ones react to the 'lead character'. Lead characters are determined by the story point, storyboard, or script. The hero of the picture will not automatically lead every scene – the lead will be taken by any character that makes the scene's story point.

Lead characters are the focal point of the scene. Their actions should be stronger and more attractive to the audience than those of the secondary characters and more interesting than the backgrounds. You do not want your audience admiring background details while dramatic action is taking place in the scene. This is a sign that the animated performance is not strong enough to sustain their attention.

Secondary characters may remain in held poses while the lead is performing an action. If the held pose is good, and the focus of the attention is elsewhere in the scene, small movements will suffice to keep the character alive. A non-animator friend once asked me why construction lines appeared on one character in an animated film. The character was in a held pose well away from the main action; unhappily, the lead character's performance did not hold my friend's attention, and a small clean-up error misdirected his eye from where he was supposed to be looking. The viewer will not notice technical errors if the animated acting keeps them involved with the story.

7.4

Equal action

Equal action on characters misdirects the audience's attention and dilutes the point of the scene.

* You see it a lot in weak animation

7.5

Focal point

The lead character must be the focal point of the scene. Audiences should not be distracted by other characters, background detail or special effects.

Staying alive

You can maintain 'life' in characters that are in held poses by using a *moving hold*. An occasional eye blink or slight tilt of the head breaks up the stillness and keeps the character 'alive' without distracting the viewer from the main action. Neglect of this important point can produce dead-eyed, unconvincing animation.

Characters in a scene should also share *eye-lines* (make eye contact) with one another if they are supposed to be working together. You may want to draw arrows from the eyes on your roughs to indicate where someone is supposed to be looking.

It is necessary to underplay the secondary character's action so that it does not upstage the lead, yet move it sufficiently so that it doesn't resemble a cardboard cut-out. In Figure 7.8 the secondary character moves enough to stay 'alive', reacting without distracting our attention from the lead. Her attention (eye contact) is fixed on the lead character and her movements are slightly delayed to indicate her thought processes and reactions to the lead's actions. The length of the delay will depend on the intelligence of the character; slower wits will have longer reaction times.

7.6

Moving hold
Characters that are held for unusually long periods of time may appear lifeless. A blink, head tilt, or slight movement (moving hold) corrects this problem.
Storyboards © 2008 by Domee Shi

7.7

Eye-lines
It is also important to have two characters that are working together share an eye-line. Diverging eye-lines indicate that the characters' attentions lie elsewhere.
Storyboards © 2008 by Domee Shi

7.8

Eye contact

Roxanne, the secondary character, makes eye contact with
the lead (Max). Her actions are understated so that they do
not upstage him. This supports the lead character's action
without distracting from it.

Thumbnails from *A Goofy Movie* by Nancy Beiman.

© Disney Enterprises, Inc.

> Think slow, act fast.
>
> – Buster Keaton, comic actor and film-maker

Oh no! He's stuck!

There, that's better!

7.9

Stock expressions
Standard or 'stock' eye expressions should be avoided.

The eyes have it

Eye expressions should reflect the character's inner thoughts and personality. Avoid using 'stock' (standard) expressions that resemble those of other animated characters. These call attention to your technique and turn your scene into an animation exercise rather than a performance. One 'look' that appears in a lot of films has the character lowering one eyebrow while raising the other as an arch smile appears on its face. This expression is turning up on so many different characters that audience members are starting to notice. Your technique should never show!

One school of 2D animation holds that 'living' lines (tracing held poses and alternating two or three of these drawings to create a constant 'boil') should be present even when drawn animated characters are in held poses. The need will vary depending on the style of the animation. Independent animator Bill Plympton uses two or three 'trace backs' to maintain the 'boil' on held poses since his rough, sketchy drawings are in a constant state of linear and textural flux and a held drawing would destroy the illusion. 2D animation with a standardised clean-up line, texture, and colour is more likely to hold a single pose or image for as long as necessary, adding secondary action to turn it into a moving hold. Timing may be identical in both techniques. The 'living line' can be seen in films such as *The Snowman* (1982).

The simplest staging for a two-character scene uses basic illustration and design principles. The lead character dominates the composition/ frame while the secondary character is in a less prominent position, as shown in the illustration from *The Snowman* (Figure 7.10). Animation literally adds another dimension to the staging since the position, scale, and character relationships may change once they begin to move within a frame that may also be in motion.

All of your films should look effortless. If the work 'shows', if somebody says, 'Isn't that a superb piece of animation', there's something wrong with what you're doing.

– Chuck Jones, lecture at the California Institute of the Arts (1976)

Direction sets the focal point

The lead character in a scene will not always be the centre of interest. A 'lead' character initiates the action in a scene; the story point sets *the centre of interest* and the *direction* determines the *focal point* and the order in which other scene elements are viewed.

The focal point of this scene from *The Snowman* (see Figure 7.10) is determined by colour contrast and the characters' eye direction as well as design elements within the layout. Our eye 'enters' the frame at screen right, first focusing on the boy. It is then directed to the snowman's face by a strong spiral composition and a 'pointer' (the tree) before being guided to the centre of interest (the cake) by the snowman's bent right arm. This direction literally takes place in less than a second, normally without our being aware of the process. (The human eye will take between four and ten frames to adjust to a new scene.) Both characters' movements are underplayed so that the staging remains consistent while the 'lead' snowman admiringly inspects the cake.

The rough drawings are where the life is.

– Bill Plympton, award-winning independent animator

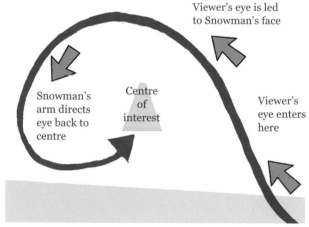

7.10

Spiral composition
Contrasts of size, position, colour emphasis and a spiral composition direct the eye from the secondary character to the lead character and then to the cake at the focal point of the scene. *The Snowman* was directed by Dianne Jackson and produced at TVC Animation.
Courtesy of TVC/The Kobal Collection

Changing character leads

Lead characters frequently change during the course of a scene. In dialogue animation, the lead often shifts between two characters who are speaking to one another. This shift should not be undertaken too abruptly unless you are animating a military review or a stagey comic exchange between a comedian and straight man. These situations are deliberately stylised and artificial and do not represent normal character interactions (see Figure 7.11).

When a secondary character assumes the lead, its body will react before it speaks or performs a significant action. The audience's attention will shift from the original lead to the new character while this action takes place. The original lead character's actions are gradually underplayed at the same time. Its actions are underplayed from then on unless it regains the lead status. The animation will then resemble natural ensemble acting rather than a game of ping-pong.

TIP

Live acting

The stilted 'ping-pong' dialogue in Figure 7.11 has one character stop moving when the other one starts to talk, calling attention to the technique. Illustration 7.12 contains more naturalistic acting as one Obvious Brother reacts and responds to the other's speech in a moving hold. This 'keeps him alive' without distracting our attention from the main figure.

'The Obvious Brothers' starring in
Bad Synchronisation

'Who was that lady I saw you
with last night?'

(Pause for laughter)

'That was no lady,
that was...'

'*...MY WIFE, YOU
MAGGOTS! NOW, DROP
AND GIVE ME 20!*'

'Sir! Yes, Sir!'

 7.11

Unsubtle lead changes
Changing leads too obviously in dialogue scenes can make
animation resemble military drills or old vaudeville routines.

I think we need
new material.

Well, I've been
thinking...

...that I should
work solo.

I'm the star of this show!

...and I'm changing my name to
'*Biff Bang!*' Do you like it?

Excuse me, but would you be
interested in a second billing and
70 mice a week?

...all right, 100
mice and top
billing!

7.12

Subtler lead change
The lead changes in the scene as the second character
responds to the first. Body action precedes the dialogue,
minimising the 'mechanical' effect.

Identical characters with different personalities

I have drawn some thumbnails showing how two identical characters with different personalities can change leads in a scene that does not contain dialogue (see Figure 7.13). Note that I am also writing the twins' names on the sketches. This keeps the identically designed characters from becoming confused in the animator's mind. The real differences become apparent when the scene is animated and contrasts in *timing* are added to the acting contrasts.

Reference footage and acting out

As with everything else in animation, there is more than one way to create the final performance. Animated character performances are often 'blocked' (staged over time) using methods that are similar, though not identical, to the ones used by live-action performers. When beginning a new project some animators first thumbnail key poses for every scene in their sequence. Others block in full-sized key poses on individual scenes without thumbnailing them first. Animators may create action footage of themselves or other people performing the action in a scene. Directors will also sometimes provide, or perform in, video acting reference. But it is sometimes impossible to act out the character movements and many things can change when the animation actually starts. Frank Thomas and Ollie Johnston wrote in *The Illusion of Life* (1981) that it is difficult to do scenes the way they are 'talked' and that things are not always done right the first time, especially when an emotional point must be made.

7.13

Nobby and Bobby
Identical twins Nobby and Bobby fight over a birthday present, changing leads as the scene progresses. The lead character is indicated in yellow. Note how the lead changes as the scene progresses.

Thumbnail your own version of a scene where three-year-old identical twins Nobby and Bobby fight over one birthday present. If you are working in CGI, use two identical characters (simple humanoids) to perform this exercise as a pose test. I recommend thumbnailing the poses in a digital program or on paper first.

➤ Twin Number One ('Nobby') is dominant and bossy.

➤ Twin Number Two ('Bobby') is quiet and stubborn.

➤ The two characters are the same size and weight.

➤ Scenario: **'The two children are fighting over one particularly appealing toy.'**

➤ Nobby and Bobby have identical designs, but they will become individuals through movement. You will indicate their contrasting personalities through their body attitudes and poses.

➤ Using my thumbnails for guidance (see Figure 7.13), thumbnail or pose two different endings for the scene of the twins and the toy.

➤ For your first ending, have **Nobby** (the **bossy** one) lead the action and win the toy.

➤ Next, thumbnail or pose an alternative ending where **Bobby** (the **stubborn** one) **leads** the action and wins the toy.

➤ You may write the twins' names on your thumbnail sketches or shade the sketches with different-coloured pencils to help plan each character's movement. (Do their actions enable you to tell the twins apart without labelling them?)

➤ Do the twins contact one another? If so, the same line of action will be used for both characters, but the acting will vary so as to maintain their individuality.

Once your thumbnails are finished, you may wish to shoot each character separately on a line tester so that you can vary the timing as necessary. Try shifting the leads by varying the timing and spacing of the key poses.

7.14 / **Line of action**
The same line of action can run through two characters' poses, showing the forces that affect both.

The acting game

Animator/director Jamaal Bradley directed the *Meet the Demoman* short and co-directed the *Meet the Spy* short with Andrew Burke and Aaron Halifax for Valve Studios' *Team Fortress 2* video game (2007). Here Jamaal describes how he uses a combination of writing, thumbnailing, and live-action reference to block the acting:

'The way that I work is a three-step process before I begin to animate. Once I have an understanding of the characters' behaviour and am fully aware of the context of the sequence I can start to plan my animation.

'*The first thing I do (if there is dialogue) is to write down word for word what is being said in my shots.* Not only do I take note of what is being said, but I also track where the *breaths* are taking place in the dialogue as well as pauses for thought.... I feel this is important because your body reacts in different ways when you are speaking and breathing. I study this until I know it verbatim.

'*The second part is thumbnailing the key poses that I want to hit*. I usually have a broad idea of how I want the acting to be so these poses let me visualise what the character will be doing before I shoot my reference. It is kind of like jotting down notes before writing a story.

'*The third step before I start pushing pixels around is shooting my reference.* This is just a loose blueprint of my acting choices. I shoot reference for a good amount of time so that I can get different choices that may go beyond my thumbnails or reinforce them.

'*The key word is "reference"*. I use [the live action] just for that. My animation may take a different shape because there will be several ideas that sprout from the footage. This may seem like a lot of planning but I have found that when you work in production you have to cut down on the amount of time you spend reworking ideas because your vision wasn't clear and completely off base from what the director and supervisor were expecting. Seventy per cent of planning will make your animation go smoother in my experience.'

– Jamaal Bradley

7.15

Storyboards block action for a video game cut scene.
Illustrations by Jamaal Bradley from *Team Fortress 2: Meet The Demoman*
© 2008 Valve Software

Give the little lady a great big hand

I have never filmed live-action reference for my own scenes since most of my characters have usually been non-human or fantastic creatures with body shapes and movements that were not possible to perform with human anatomy. However, I often use my arms, fingers and hands as 'puppets' in order to block character movements within a scene and provide rough timing for my animation. Human hands and fingers are extremely flexible. They are capable of moving faster than the rest of the body and can more easily represent the limber and stylised movement of animated characters. This technique also allows the animator to 'act out' a dialogue scene between two characters in real time. Other animators use similar methods; Ellen Woodbury raised and lowered her shoulders while seated at her animation desk to time the movement of animal characters. The 'acting out' takes place largely in the animator's imagination, which transcends the limitations of the body.

It is not necessary to film the movement of your own hands; these performers are literally an arm's length away from you at all times. The actions, arcs, and timing may be repeated as often as needed. Broad actions are blocked and thumbnailed first. Secondary and overlapping action can be pantomimed and added as the scene develops.

As you can see, animation acting styles differ as much as animated design does. You may find that one method of blocking and staging your scenes works well in all instances, or you may use a combination of several methods. It is not necessary to adhere to a specific design or acting 'method' or formula since this can produce formulaic, predictable acting. Techniques used in animation are a means to an end, not the end itself. The animated caricature of reality has created many believable characters with individual personalities. Equally believable characters and personalities have been created from objects as simple as a Luxo lamp, a dot and a line. The animator's objective is to create living, believable character performances using a medium that enables a human artist/actor to perform any character that can be drawn, designed or built. Never let your technique become more important than the acting in your scene or film.

Next >

Let us now consider ensemble acting in animated film.

Changing leads in multiple-character scenes

'We sometimes had as many as two characters in our crowd scenes.'

– Isidore 'Friz' Freleng, Warner Brothers director

There is an old joke about a theatrical troupe that was forced to make budgetary cutbacks due to lack of funding. As a result, their new production had to be re-titled *Snow White and the Two Dwarfs*.

Animated film-makers frequently eliminate unnecessary characters while the film is being storyboarded, usually after the project is up on Leica (story) reels and the film's final running time is established. This is the most efficient way to avoid wasting time animating footage and characters that will later be cut from the picture. Sometimes two characters may be combined into one at this stage. It is doubtful whether you will be able to reduce the size of your main cast if the story is about three bears, four Marx brothers, or 'The Magnificent Seven'.

So, before starting layout and animation on films with large casts, it is a good idea to inspect your storyboards carefully and consider the following points:

- ✎ Where are group and crowd scenes needed in this project? (They should always make a story point – let there be a reason for them to be there.)

- ✎ Which group scenes can be shortened or eliminated?

- ✎ Which scenes can be restaged with fewer characters?

- ✎ Could you use two-shots and close-ups of a few characters to contrast with the group shots? This can give the audience some key figures to follow within the group.

- ✎ Can layout and design imply the existence of the group so that fewer characters can be used in the scene?

- ✎ Crowd scenes (groups of anonymous characters that may appear only in one or two scenes, known in animation as 'incidentals') should be considered a special effect since they do not often get to act. Blocking crowd action will be discussed in the 'Potemkin villages' section of this chapter.

There is a trick to animating groups of characters that is roughly summarised in Friz Freleng's quote at the top of this page: *Not every member of the group is equally important.*

Two or three dominant characters may trade leads and carry most of the acting while the rest of the group assumes 'supporting' roles that rarely have them as the centre of interest. This technique is evident in most of the dwarfs' scenes in *Snow White and the Seven Dwarfs*; Doc, Dopey, and Grumpy are the three leading characters in the group and they handle the lion's share of the storytelling. Sneezy, Happy, Bashful and Sleepy (who naturally has the least to do) play secondary roles in most scenes, though there are exceptions – notably when Sneezy sneezes. Scenes with all seven dwarfs together appear mostly in the sequence where they march home and search for an intruder in the house; as we get to know their personalities, two shots and three shots become more prevalent and there are fewer large group scenes. Similarly, Patch, Penny, Lucky, Freckles, Pepper and Rolly carry most of the acting for the puppies in *One Hundred and One Dalmatians* (1961).

Goldilocks and the One Bear

7.16

Goldilocks and the One Bear
Some stories with a numbered cast of characters cannot be simplified or condensed without losing credibility.

Our crowd: The animated ensemble

The Three Fates in *Hercules*, which I animated, shifted leads when each character spoke a line. Their personalities were simultaneously malignant and funny and didn't change during the course of the picture, so their scenes emphasised bizarre sight gags with all three sisters taking turns as the centre of interest.

In one scene the background characters deliberately upstaged the lead. Clotho (the Fate with the long chin and scraggy hair) is speaking in the foreground, attempting to sound very threatening and mysterious while doing witchy things with her arms. Her sister Lachesis (she with the long arms and nose, who is standing behind Clotho) picks up the Fates' solitary eye while it is still lodged in one-eyed sister Atropos' head. Lachesis shakes the eye loose, causing Atropos to fall to the ground like an old sock while Clotho finishes her line *'We know EVERYTHING!'* Clotho is performing one big evenly timed action with her arms at this point (based on a gesture that voice actress Amanda Plummer performed at her recording session). The audience's attention is deliberately diverted from the lead character to the more interesting and differently timed background action. Clotho ceases to lead the scene when Lachesis makes her move.

Normally, dramatic characters are not upstaged by other characters in the scene, but exceptions do occur. In *Snow White and the Seven Dwarfs*, the princess picks wildflowers and plays with a bird as the huntsman approaches her from behind with an unsheathed knife. The scene is staged so that we are looking at the girl's unprotected back as the shadow of the knife enters at screen right and hovers over her. Snow White is leading the action, but our attention is focused on that steadily advancing menace. Director Alfred Hitchcock used similar staging in *Dial M for Murder* (1954); see Figure 7.18.

As with the two-shots discussed earlier in this chapter, the lead in a group scene shifts from one character to another gradually to avoid a mechanical or 'ping-pong' effect. I normally draw lines of action for group scenes to show where the momentum of the animation is going. I use these lines of action to block the placement of all the characters in the scene.

204   7. DOUBLE TIMING: ANIMATING CHARACTER INTERACTIONS

< Staging and composition · Changing leads in multiple-character scenes · Potemkin villages: Crowd scenes and how to fake them >

7.17

Lead characters upstaged again

A lead character in the foreground may be upstaged by secondary characters performing more interesting action in the background. This is extremely effective when used in comedy.

Poster from the Library of Congress

7.18

Dial M for Murder

A dramatic scene may also see a lead character upstaged if the story requires it. Grace Kelly is the lead in this scene, but our attention is directed to the menacing intruder behind her.

Courtesy of Warner Bros/The Kobal Collection

The animated duet

Here are two sheets of thumbnails that I drew for a scene in *A Goofy Movie* (1995) where Max and Goofy fight over a cardboard cut-out of rock star 'Powerline' (see Figures 7.19 and 7.20). The cut-out, though inanimate, was handled as a third character in the scene. The first sketch contains my notes, which describe the point of the scene and shows the line of action that runs through all three characters. Goofy leads the action until Max runs into the scene and grabs the other end of the cut-out, whereupon neither he nor Goofy lead since the opposing forces affecting them are roughly equal.

The second set of thumbnails breaks this action down further so that you see Max's line of action separate from Goofy's as he breaks free. Max now takes the lead while saying the line, *'Oh Dad! You ruined it!'* Goofy is underplayed while Max says his line, and then re-assumes the lead as he responds, *'Sorry about that. Who* was *he, anyway?'* Max then anticipates a line that he will deliver in close-up in the next scene.

A few scenes later, Goofy attempts to dance the Mambo with Max, who doesn't want to participate. Max fights Goofy every inch of the way and eventually breaks free to run offscreen. Goofy leads the action; these thumbnails are for the first part of the scene. Max's struggles, though violent, cannot break him away from the line of action that is running through both characters. Max's action does not have any effect on Goofy, who is larger and stronger. Only his hands are affected as Max attempts to dislodge his grip. Eventually Max does escape and the lines of action for the two characters separate. Goofy maintains the lead and reacts only after Max has left the scene.

I work on all characters simultaneously when animating this type of group shot, though the lead will have the keys set down first. The story point *(Goofy is unaware that Max doesn't want to dance with him)* determines how the animation will be handled *(Goofy always leads and Max's struggles have no effect on him)*.

After the keys for Goofy are set I add Max's keys (modifying Goofy's arms to work with him). I then add breakdowns for both characters at the same time, working on a section of the action (either a phrase of dialogue or a complete movement within the scene – here, it might be one or two dance steps). Once again, I start with the lead character and then provide breakdowns for the secondary character. Once that section's breakdowns are done, I move on to the next section. Some animators do breakdowns for the entire scene rather than working in sections. Others work on one character at a time. There is no right or wrong way; use whichever method works for the scene and for you.

Goofy's action was easier to animate than Max's since he moved to a musical beat and used pre-planned dance steps. Max's movements were 'wild' but he still moved in time with Goofy until he broke free.

Goofy's dance was based on a rather silly musical number I found in a dated French live-action musical. I sketched the foot patterns of one dancer and made another sketch of a foolish movement of the dancer's hands; this was one of the few times that I have used live-action reference for a scene! I also used reference footage for a scene of villain Cat R. Waul saying *'WHAT?'* to John Cleese's voice track for *An American Tail: Fievel Goes West* (Amblimation, 1991). I studied footage of Cleese saying the line and then put it away and animated the scene incorporating Cleese's characteristic shoulder lift into the animation. It's necessary to use filmed reference when I must duplicate a specific action; but most of the time I reference memories from past film viewings, my imagination and my sketchbooks.

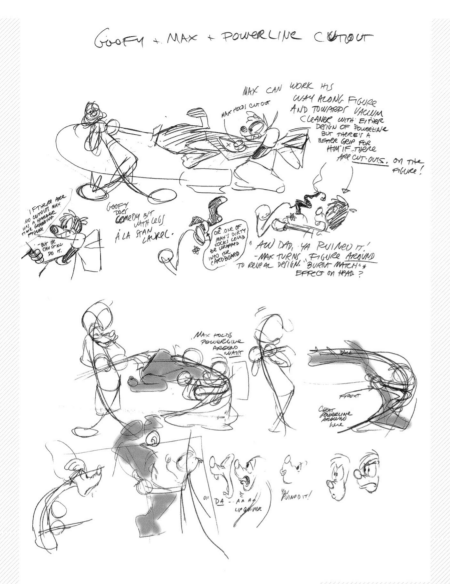

GOOFY + MAX + POWERLINE CUTOUT

MAX HOLDS CUTOUT

MAX CAN WORK HIS
WAY ALONG FIGURE
AND TOWARDS VACUUM
CLEANER WITH EITHER
DESIGN OF POWERLINE
BUT THERE'S A
BETTER GRIP FOR
HIM IF THERE
ARE CUT-OUTS ON THE
FIGURE!

"IF THERE ARE
NO CUTOUTS MAX
HAS A HARDER
TIME GRABBING
FIGURE"

GOOFY
DOES
COMEDY B/T
WITH LEGS
À LA STAN
LAUREL.

"BUT HE
CAN STILL
DO IT.

OR ONE OF
MAX'S DIRTY
SOCKS COULD
BE WRAPPED
INTO THE
CARDBOARD

"AW DAD, YA RUINED IT!"
- MAX TURNS FIGURE AROUND
TO REVEAL DESIGN. "BURNT MATCH"
EFFECT ON HEAD?

MAX HOLDS
POWERLINE
AROUND
WAIST

BACK

FRONT

GREAT
POWERLINE
AROUND
HERE

OH DA---AAA
LIP QUIVER

YA
RUINED IT!

7.19

Character groups

Lines of action block the movement of character groups throughout the scene. The three characters in the first sketch (one of them a cardboard cut-out) share the same line of action, and none lead. In the second sketch Max breaks away from the group and takes over the lead in the scene.

A Goofy Movie animation by Nancy Beiman, © Disney Enterprises, Inc.

7.20

Goofy and Max

Goofy was thumbnailed first, and then Max's poses were added following the same line of action. Different-coloured pencils keep the characters separate.

A Goofy Movie animation by Nancy Beiman, © Disney Enterprises, Inc.

Triple timing

It is very important to vary the timing on the characters in group scenes even if they are sharing a line of action and even if the action is very quick. A character that abruptly takes the lead from another in an argument (see Figure 7.21) will anticipate their action before doing so. Dialogue can also overlap, smoothing the transition. Note how the prop helps direct our eye from one character to another, though the lead may shift to a character that does *not* have the prop. Although the three characters move throughout the entire scene, they alternate the lead role, which keeps the scene's staging clear.

Sylvain Chomet's *The Triplets of Belleville* (2003) uses a different type of ensemble acting. The three sisters function as a unit, with none taking a dominant role. They usually appear together and take turns leading scenes, but in a less obvious manner than the Seven Dwarfs do. In the famous 'frog dinner' scene, Violette, Blanche, and Rose happily chow down while the nauseated Madame Souza watches in the foreground (see Figure 7.22). Our attention shifts from one sister to the other, moving from screen left to screen right. Close-ups of each character follow the group shots to show details of the action.

Sisters Satsuki and Mei are the main characters of Hayao Miyazaki's *My Neighbour Totoro* (1988) and we experience the film's world through their eyes. Many scenes feature groups of characters with wildly different sizes and designs. The sisters, both dominant characters, are usually the leads even in scenes that feature the huge O Totoro. In this scene colour accents and dynamic poses draw our attention to the girls; the Totoro are in neutral poses (see Figure 7.23). The eye will be drawn to strong actions, colour, or design. The size of the character is not the dominant factor in establishing the lead or focal point of a scene.

So, while there is no one set way to handle groups of characters, there are many different techniques that can be used to achieve the result that you desire and the scene requires.

Yellow accent indicates lead character

We start with Kit. Pig enters scene (Kit is still leading action)

1   2

Lead shifts to pig

3

4

Pig is leading

Wak enters scene

5

Lead shifts to Wak

6

Pig in moving hold

Wak is leading, others are in moving holds

7

Lead shifts again to Kit as Wak flies out

8

Scene ends with Pig leading and Kit in moving hold

9

7.21

Directing the eye
Important props help to direct the eye but don't always stay with the lead character.

208   7. DOUBLE TIMING: ANIMATING CHARACTER INTERACTIONS

< Staging and composition · Changing leads in multiple-character scenes · Potemkin villages: Crowd scenes and how to fake them >

7.22

The Triplets of Belleville

The Triplets of Belleville function as a unit, with no one character emphasised more than the other two. The viewer's eye is led from one character to the other by staging, colour, and animated action.

The Triplets of Belleville © 2003 Sony Pictures Classics and The Kobal Collection

7.23

My Neighbour Totoro

The human children in *My Neighbour Totoro* lead the action in this group shot with the Totoro clan.

© Aftokuma Enterprises and The Kobal Collection

Pig
two legged

Kit
four legged

Wak
wings

7.24

Introducing Pig, Kit and Wak
Three different-sized characters will work together
in the next exercise.

Pig is frustrated
and angry

Kit is surprised
and hurt – cries

Waah

Wak is smug, proud
– a winner

7.25

Motivation and acting
Character motivation and acting creates a story in a
standard animation exercise.

Use the three characters in the illustrations opposite or **simple** designs of your own to thumbnail the following actions:

Part 1

➤ Three characters try to reach an object that is out of their reach on a high shelf. Use a simple layout and design a prop on the shelf (your choice). A ladder may or may not be available (maybe it is on the shelf?).

➤ In the first version, have the characters work together to retrieve the object. They like one another though they may have a friendly rivalry.

➤ Block the body action first, add expressions afterward. Watch your eye-lines – friendly characters will make eye contact with one another.

➤ **Do not stage all action in one scene.** Thumbnail a short sequence starting with an establishing shot and then staging the action using a variety of two-shots, close-ups, and group shots where they are needed. Tell the story in the most interesting way possible.

➤ Concentrate on acting; develop a personality for each character.

➤ Decide whether one character leads or if leads change during the scene and draw thumbnails showing how they do, or do not, reach the object (your choice).

➤ **It's best to draw story beats for the ending first.** Sketch several possible endings, pick the one that you like best, and then work backwards, drawing thumbnails showing how they got there.

➤ Different coloured pencils may be used for the characters though it's not required.

➤ Can they balance on one another's shoulders? Is there a prop that can help them reach the object on the shelf?

➤ Is one character doing more work than the others?

➤ Does one character want the object more than the other two?

➤ The least imaginative staging is in a single scene with the characters simply getting the object. Go for an imaginative interpretation!

Part 2

➤ Now thumbnail a second version where the characters do NOT get along with one another. They are competing for the object.

➤ Is one character trying to prevent the other two from getting the object? Or do two of them team up to prevent the third one from winning the prize?

➤ Might one character prefer to destroy the object rather than let the other two have it?

➤ What about eye contact? Characters that do not like one another may not even want to **look** at each other.

➤ Compare the two sets of thumbnails. Was it more difficult to block the action for characters that did **not** work together?

Next >

In the next section we will see how very large groups of characters can be reduced to a minimum in more ways than one.

Potemkin villages: Crowd scenes and how to fake them

Potemkin village: An elaborate construction that provides a false front or façade: after Grigori Aleksandrovich Potemkin, who it is said built fake villages to deceive Empress Catherine the Great about his accomplishments.

Animated films were once so expensive to produce that few featured the 'cast of thousands' that appeared in some contemporary live-action pictures. The Xerox process, when adapted for animation at the Walt Disney studio, made it possible to animate groups of characters economically by reusing and resizing animation, resulting in *One Hundred and One Dalmatians* ('Our studio would have found it difficult to animate ONE spotted dog', Chuck Jones once quipped.) Usually animated crowds only appeared in a few shots consisting of repeated cycles. Sometimes the crowds were implied; a jar of *'10,000 Instant Martians'* (a believable and clever shortcut) appeared, reconstituted, as feathery topknots poking through New York City's sewers and streets at the end of Chuck Jones' *Hare-Way to the Stars* (1958). The audience already knew what the Martians looked like since three identical specimens had been chasing Bugs Bunny throughout the picture (making the Martians identical was another clever shortcut). The appearance of the other 9,997 Martians was left to the imagination but since the sprouting topknots were identical with those of the original three, the audience could easily 'see' the teeming hordes with the aid of this onscreen hint. If the film was produced today a computer program would make it possible for all 10,000 Martians to appear in the last scene, but I think that the understated version is much funnier than a literal representation would be. Director Chuck Jones, layout man Maurice Noble, and story man Mike Maltese took a limitation (no budget or production time for crowd scenes) and turned it into one of the picture's strengths.

7.26

Hand-drawn and digital animation
Computer-animated cyclists are combined with a hand-drawn digitally painted crowd and background in Sylvain Chomet's *The Triplets of Belleville*.
© 2003 Sony Pictures Classics and The Kobal Collection

New solutions and new problems

Animated features and short films in all media have benefited from the use of computer technology. Programs have become cheap enough, and computers fast enough, to allow artists working outside the studio system to create their films with industry-quality tools. Computer technology also makes it possible to produce animated films with large casts in the same time period that it once took to produce simpler films.

Animation is easier to produce now (and should also be *cheaper* to produce now) than at any time since the days of silent film. Yet animated films can still run into financial and deadline problems because of poor planning and over-production. (Computer-animated crowd scenes can get very expensive!) The computer cannot serve as a crutch; it, and all technology, is only the means to an end. Animated film-makers should not assume that something can be 'fixed in post'.

Crowd scenes can be the downfall of an overly ambitious production. Careful planning in pre-production (design and storyboard) and the use of group and crowd scenes only *where they are needed* will allow you to conserve and properly allocate the most important parts of your animated budget: your *time* and your *health*, both physical and financial.

It is not strictly accurate to refer to 'traditional' and 'computer' animation media any more since several different animation techniques are now frequently seamlessly blended in one motion picture. For example, three-dimensional characters, props, and backgrounds interact with hand-drawn, digitally painted characters and scene elements in Sylvain Chomet's film *The Triplets of Belleville* (2003).

7.27

Stylised substitutions
Animated films use stylised substitutions for crowd scenes to save production time and stay within their budgets.
Bollywood Baby © 2007 by Nancy Beiman

Simplification and finding the essence of the scene

On some animated films the director and head of layout would review the layouts for a sequence about to go into production in what was known as a 'simplification pass'. The simplification pass modified the layouts so that a crowd could be created with fewer characters than the original staging may have included. In one instance the number of characters in a scene was reduced from 100 to 20 without losing the 'feel' of the crowd scene.

Some crowd sequences, such as the wildebeest stampede in *The Lion King* (1994) or the charge of the Huns in *Mulan* (1998), are essential to the story. Both were created by animating two or three different cycle runs on one CGI character and duplicating them hundreds of times to create the charging hordes. It was not important to show the personalities of the characters in these crowds; they represented an irresistible force, not individuals. The timing on the runs was offset so that footfalls did not all hit at the same time and they did not all run at the same speed, which avoided a mechanical look.

In *The Lion King*, Simba and Mufasa were the lead characters and the centre of interest during the wildebeest stampede. Scenes are staged at their eye level so that we identify with the danger of their situation. *Mulan's* charging Huns were sometimes seen from an eagle-eye view; the nameless characters embodied the brutality and impersonality of a military invasion.

Staging is an important component of successful animation (and not just in crowd scenes). Even if it is now much easier to generate huge crowds in CGI-animated films than was formerly the case, the crowd and spectacle cannot carry the picture's story. The audience must be directed to the lead characters, take an interest in their predicament, and care about what happens to them.

a. Too busy

b. Simplified

7.28

Simplification
A simplification pass reduces the number and complexity of crowd scenes while retaining the sequence's story points and character interactions.
The Stressful Adventures of Boxhead and Roundhead
© 2009 by Elliot Cowan

Characters may be included in a crowd

Staging can create or intensify motion within a crowd scene, as shown in the example from *The Snowman* (see Figure 7.29). Our attention is first drawn to the snowman at screen left who is separated from the others by the piano. The eye then follows a spiral (with the piano acting as a 'pointer') down toward the snowman seated at the keyboard and loops around to the right, allowing us to view the three remaining snowmen in a particular order before ending back at the piano player.

The spiral composition draws us into the scene and creates a friendly atmosphere which is intensified by the warm colour palette and the snowmen's gazes, which are also directed inward; some are making eye contact. All of this takes an instant to view and we are not conscious of how our gaze is directed while watching the film, yet much careful planning went into the staging of this scene so that all elements and characters are viewed in precisely the order that the director wished us to view them.

The crowd scene from *The Triplets of Belleville* (see Figure 7.30) shows a champion cyclist who has just won the Tour de France. His slight figure is flanked by two very large women; seven photographers surround the central group in a circular composition. The women fill most of the central area in the frame and are a crowd in themselves, so there is no need to have other figures standing behind them. A large tarpaulin the same colour as the women's dresses appears at the top of the frame and, with them, creates a three-sided 'picture frame'. The excellent staging gives the impression that there are many other characters milling about just out of camera range; sound effects and popping flashbulbs will add to the confused effect. The main characters in this scene did not have to move much since they are posing for the photographers. The animation of the audience was underplayed yet gave the impression of a scene filled with hectic action. No one makes eye contact with anyone else; everyone is looking at the cameras. The central character is deliberately dwarfed by his companions and the milling crowd.

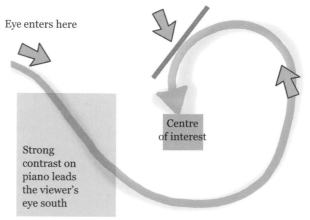

Bow is also a 'pointer' leading eye to centre of interest

Eye enters here

Centre of interest

Strong contrast on piano leads the viewer's eye south

7.29

The Snowman
This scene from *The Snowman* uses a spiral to lead our eye around the frame, creating motion within the composition even before the characters start animating.
© TVC/The Kobal Collection

7.30

The Triplets of Belleville
This crowd did not need to move much.
The layout and colour direct the eye to the central figures.
The Triplets of Belleville © 2003 Sony Pictures Classics and The Kobal Collection

Characters may be excluded from a crowd

In this scene from *The Triplets of Belleville* (see Figure 7.31) the small figures of Madame Souza and her dog Bruno are overwhelmed by the hulking citizens of Belleville. The scene is staged in an upshot so that the crowd characters are visually compared to the skyscrapers behind them. Here, as in the earlier scene from this picture, no character makes eye contact with another. Each eye-line is directed to a different point outside the border of the frame, which isolates each individual from the other characters in the scene. Even Bruno the dog is staring at nothing. Madame Souza, the lead character, looks directly at the audience and the composition (one-point perspective with all lines converging where she is standing) draws our gaze toward her. However, she is pretending to be blind so we cannot read her expression. The scene's staging produces a cold, fragmented, alienating effect.

Graphic animation

We have seen how creative staging and colour can create the impression of a crowd so that the animator does not have to literally portray large groups of characters onscreen. But there will be times when crowds must move, and perhaps move violently. Here is a process that will make animating crowd scenes (often referred to as an 'animator's nightmare') easier.

Instead of attempting to draw each individual in the crowd on the first pass, you can plan basic movement and time the action by thumbnailing poses of a graphic shape that represents the volume of all characters in the crowd. In effect, the crowd characters are combined into one massive shape that follows one line of action. The graphic shape will change its outline to indicate how the crowd progresses through the scene. Its volume can stretch and deform as much as necessary, depending on the uniformity of the character movement. The graphic outline of a disciplined army marching in ranks will distort less than one representing a pack of terrified pigs escaping from a pen. Write down the type of movement the crowd must perform (symmetrical? fragmented?) before creating the graphic. Then draw your thumbnails.

Next, a few smaller graphic symbols are animated within the larger shape to represent groups of characters within the crowd. Then, smaller symbols are added that represent individuals within these groups. The *last* thing the animator does is draw the details of individual crowd characters. Crowd movements can therefore be timed before the characters are actually drawn.

So a crowd is not an easy assignment, but if the scene is constructed in this fashion you will have less chance of encountering the very worst 'animation nightmare' of them all:

Making corrections on a crowd scene!

7.31

One-point perspective
Madam Souza and Bruno the dog lead the action but are not part of the lonely crowd.
The Triplets of Belleville © 2003 Sony Pictures Classics and The Kobal Collection

One of my mantras on Beavis and Butthead was instructing board and layout artists not to let BG characters 'intrude' on our stars. I didn't even want BG characters to SMILE – that's how little acting I wanted on them! I know that's extreme, but it worked in this case…. In general, my favourite crowds are the ones that are offscreen and done with SFX only!

Yvette Kaplan, animation director, *Beavis and Butthead Do America* (1996)

1. The action is first blocked and timed for the silhouette of the group.
A graphic shape represents the volume of the crowd.
The movement of the mass is thumbnailed and timed first.

2. Smaller, labelled silhouettes and colour are added
to indicate specific characters.

3. Individual movements and arcs within the group shape may differ.
Here 'Peg' anticipates up while the others move downwards.

7.32

Smaller elements
The graphic shape is broken down into smaller and smaller
elements until the action and timing is set. Character details
are added last.

7.33

Additional characters
Additional characters may be added to break
up the 'mass' feeling.

8

Character development over time

An animated character develops a character arc by learning a life lesson, realising an error, overcoming an obstacle or discovering its own inner strength. The difference between the character arc and story arc is explained here. A character's inner development is not restricted by medium or the length of the film; we will analyse and compare arcs from features, short films and television series.

The chapter, and the book, ends with a look at the future of video games – a medium in which the player also functions as a character.

And for the grand finale...

Character and story arcs

'I brought in the stories many times. I don't just do animation.'

– Ray Harryhausen, film producer, special effects artist and animator

Some characters never change. Their constancy can be reassuring. The 'Three Stooges' fail at everything they try and we always know what is going to happen to them before it happens. The surprise in their films, which develop in a similar way to 'Roadrunner and Coyote' cartoons, comes from varying the incompetence. The Coyote always reacts to situations in a consistent way. Tragedies can also be built around characters that cannot or will not change. Captain Ahab in *Moby Dick* (1851) is just as fixated and, in a way, just as incompetent as Wile E. Coyote. All of these characters are influenced by the *story arc* that sets the goal they seek to achieve and affects all characters in the film. However, they never develop a *character arc* that reflects their emotional growth since they remain the same at the end of the story as they were in the beginning.

A character arc may be an *internal* transformation that is sparked by any of the following:

✎ A sudden realisation of error.

✎ The revelation of inner strength and character when under pressure.

✎ A determination to change their ways either on their own initiative or by heeding the advice of another character.

In animation, internal changes may also be represented or accompanied by the literal, *external* transformation of the animated performer. Both types will be discussed in this chapter.

Everything originates with the story. Here, Yvette Kaplan explains how story arcs and character arcs develop at the same time:

'I liken constructing a believable and compelling character arc for an animated character to building a house of cards. One false move and, *whoosh!* – it all falls apart. That's why we were so zealous about getting it right during Story on *Ice Age*. Our characters not only had to be funny and entertaining, as do all animated feature stars, they had to travel *huge* distances emotionally; we had death, heartbreak, betrayal, murder, self-sacrifice, love and redemption – and this was a *comedy*! We had three characters who *just* met, yet who needed to bond enough to risk their lives for each other, *and* the baby they were transporting, while hiding crucial truths from each other – and the audience!

'To complicate matters, Manny (the mammoth) had a doozy of a back story that needed to be revealed delicately, as did all the story points, at just the right times and in just the right places. Since things that read well in a script don't always ring true once the visualisation starts, once that performance is up on the pitch board, we were always re-evaluating, always questioning. Of course we all knew we weren't making a tragedy, we needed gags too. But if a gag risked breaking a character's finely built arc, if just one line or action felt false, we had more to lose than a laugh. We'd lose our audience.'

– Yvette Kaplan, head of story on *Ice Age* (2002)

Epiphanies and transformations

Originally a religious experience, epiphanies now refer to a character's change of behaviour, or realisation of error, or sudden comprehension of what is going on around them. Epiphanies are about sudden spiritual change but like 'overnight' success, they can take a long time to achieve.

Novelist William S. Burroughs, in the introduction to his novel *Naked Lunch* (1959), called an epiphany 'a frozen moment when everyone sees what is at the end of every fork'.

A dramatic epiphany occurs in *Pinocchio* (1940) when the hero receives news that his father Geppetto is in danger. Pinocchio immediately takes off to rescue the old man without a thought for his own safety.

Until that time Pinocchio has been a weak character. He is a naïve, easily influenced 'puppet' in more ways than one, following the advice of the bad characters he meets while ignoring the advice of his 'conscience', Jiminy Cricket. After his epiphany Pinocchio's character is transformed. *This is the definition of a character arc.*

Pinocchio becomes a brave and resourceful character who can think for himself and consider the needs of others. He no longer needs help from the Blue Fairy or Jiminy Cricket. All of his heroic deeds are the result of his newfound bravery and unselfishness, two qualities that the Blue Fairy told him he needed to prove *and that were always present in his character*. Pinocchio rescues Geppetto and ultimately completes his character arc when his wooden body is transformed into that of a real boy. He undergoes both *internal* and *external* transformation.

Similarly, after seeing his father's ghost in *The Lion King*, Simba has an epiphany that causes him to abandon his self-indulgent life and return to Pride Rock to defeat his wicked uncle and assume his adult responsibilities. Simba's character arc develops suddenly when he realises his own inner strength and understands that his kingdom needs him. He undergoes an *internal* transformation. There is no external one.

Mr Magoo knew that he was nearsighted but was too vain to wear glasses. He has an epiphany in one film, realising his error in a scene beautifully animated by Art Babbitt, as he recalled in our interview in 1979:

'There was one picture we worked on – I forget the name of it [*Fuddy Duddy Buddy*, 1951] – but in this short, Magoo played tennis with a walrus. He had mistaken this walrus for a friend of his. There is one scene where Magoo is very, very sad – he realises he's made a terrible mistake. But then he pulls himself out of that mood right after that and says, "Well, *even* if you're a Walrus... Walrus, you're a *friend* of mine."'

In the 'sad scene' Babbitt refers to, Magoo is told that his tennis partner is a walrus who is being returned to the zoo. Magoo rants in protest, waving a fish which he believes is a tennis racquet, but suddenly realises the truth. He stops mid-rant and wipes away a tear from one eye with a small sigh. He then tosses aside the fish, delivers Babbitt's line, and stomps off to free his friend.

Unusually, Magoo is *not* transformed by his epiphany. He is the same cheerfully obstinate and nearsighted character at the end of the film that he was at the beginning. But there was that one scene where we suddenly saw him understand his weakness.

An idol is revealed to have feet of clay in L. Frank Baum's *The Wonderful Wizard of Oz* (1900) when the Great Oz is revealed (by a dog!) to be a mere showman operating theatrical props. The wizard must use simple charms to convince Dorothy's companions, the Cowardly Lion, Tin Woodman and Scarecrow, that they actually achieved their respective goals of courage, a heart and brains. All three characters developed dramatic character arcs during the story that proved they already possessed these qualities – *but none of them had an epiphany*, so they never became aware of this. Only external evidence could convince the Lion, Scarecrow, and Tin Man that internal change had occurred.

Epiphanies should build on what we already know about the character and not spring from thin air.

An epiphany is *always* internal; while it may be inspired by another character's advice, it cannot be imposed from outside.

Journeys and endings

A character arc is sometimes defined as a 'hero's journey'. This may be physical (a quest or mission) or emotional (overcoming a personal weakness). Both types of arc affect the character of Frodo Baggins in J. R. R. Tolkien's *The Lord of the Rings* (1954). Frodo is an ordinary hobbit who becomes a hero against his will when he is assigned the care and disposal of the 'One Ring of Power'. His character arc develops simultaneously with that of his colleague Sam Gamgee during a long and dangerous journey. Sam, another ordinary hobbit, becomes a hero through his selfless love for his friend. Gandalf the wizard and Galadriel the elf queen are mentors who help Frodo along the way. Frodo is menaced by external demons personified in the Black Riders, but his conflicts are both spiritual and physical. (Significantly, a knife wound inflicted by the Riders endangers Frodo's soul more than his body.) Gollum, originally a villain, helps them while also developing a strong character arc. Like Dr Jekyll, Gollum embodies his inner evil in a separate persona which he literally fights to overcome. Frodo succumbs to evil at the end of his journey and announces that he will keep, not destroy, the ring in a sort of *anti-*epiphany. Ironically it is Gollum who helps Frodo complete his mission. At the end of the story the otherworldly Frodo cannot resume his old life and literally departs for another world.

The successive stages of the 'Hero's Journey' have been adequately described elsewhere. It is one way of setting a character arc. Some other ways include:

- *External change.* Actual physical transformation can bring about changes in character, as with the Frog Prince or Shrek's Princess Fiona.

- Internal change by discovery or realisation (an epiphany). Simba and Pinocchio both develop emotional maturity and a sense of responsibility when others are endangered. Bolt and Buzz Lightyear both discover that they do not really have super-powers but display true heroism in other ways.

- Influence from another. One character arc may be influenced by another's. For example, 'Lady' becomes braver and more adventurous when she meets 'Tramp' and he becomes respectable due to her influence; 'Beast' and 'Beauty' are transformed (in his case, literally) by their love for each other.

- Change of setting. Arcs may also develop when the hero must adjust to a new and unfamiliar environment. This last situation is known as a *'fish-out-of-water'* story and is used in many animated films and stories. *Kung Fu Panda* (2008) and *Ratatouille* (2007) are both excellent examples and *The Lord of the Rings'* 'hobbit' characters are all 'fish out of water'.

- Character arcs can be influenced by a combination of these elements, for example *Ice Age*, *Bolt* and *Toy Story* are heroes' journeys that are also fish-out-of-water stories. There are many similar examples.

Although events will influence behaviour, successful character arcs should appear to originate in the animated performer's own thought processes and not be totally dependent on external circumstances. The seed of change must be present before emotional and spiritual growth occurs.

Watch an animated film (it may be a short film, television programme, or feature), the length does not matter as long as it has a self-contained, linear story.

After you have viewed the film, write notes analysing the following points:

➤ How do the lead characters change during the course of the film? How many develop a strong character arc?

 If there appears to be no change, explain why you believe this to be so. For example: Wile E. Coyote never learns that malfunctioning technology from the Acme Corporation will not help him catch the Road Runner. This reveals a flaw in the coyote's character. Chuck Jones explained the coyote's behaviour with a quote from George Santayana that 'fanaticism is redoubling your effort when you have forgotten your aim' (goal). The Coyote cannot learn from his mistakes since he persists in believing that THIS time, the technology **will** work.

➤ Are the character developments convincing? Do you remain interested in what happens to the leads, or do secondary characters become more interesting?

➤ Do the lead characters' arcs influence secondary characters, or vice versa?

➤ Do any of the characters undergo an epiphany? Is it believable? Does it result in a change of behaviour? Describe this change.

➤ If you are using a television series for this exercise, pick one episode and analyse how much of the character's response depends on your knowledge of its behaviour in previous episodes. Could someone who has never watched the programme before understand the characters' motivations after viewing this single episode?

Well, nobody's perfect

Perfection can be boring. Your animated characters should have some elements in their characters that 'humanise' them and make them interesting to watch. They should not win all the time or perform every action flawlessly. This ensures that the audience remains interested in finding out whether they succeed. If a character is invincible there is no conflict or development in its character or the story. Superman is a heroic character that was originally designed without a character arc. He was born invincible and fought criminals. (He always won.) Superman had no inner demons to overcome; his conflicts were entirely external. Superman's creators provided Kryptonite to kill him or at least slow him down. But Kryptonite, like Medusa's gaze, could be avoided; it did not affect Superman's character. Later writers decided to give Superman some character flaws that would create some interest in his stories. These could be a little extreme. Superman became a murderer, betrayed his friends, cheated on Lois Lane and, in *The Bride of Jungle Jimmy*, dressed as a witch doctor and forced Jimmy Olsen to 'marry' a giant ape. These variations totally changed Superman's original character, and many additional 'negative characteristics' were tried over the years. Superman has been re-imagined and resurrected numerous times and is no longer portrayed as a perfect being. Examples of Superman behaving badly can be found at <http://www.superdickery.com>.

Spiderman and Batman were designed with human character flaws. Like Frodo, they became inadvertent heroes.

Villainous characters can be the lead characters and maintain audience interest. Shrek the Ogre becomes a hero in spite of himself, and despite his protestations of evil, he is always a very likable character. Other villainous leads feature in *Despicable Me* (2010), *The Emperor's New Groove* (2000), and other (mainly modern) animated films.

Character development in feature films

Character arcs are necessary in longer animated films since we must remain involved with the animated actors for an hour or more. They keep the audience interested in what happens to the protagonists and, in some cases, lead it to identify with the animated actors.

Features can spend between two and five years in pre-production and development. There is time to explore character personalities and experiment with how they interact with other characters.

I would like to end this section with some quotes from Disney animator/director Ward Kimball. Kimball's comments indicate some of the thought processes that animators use when developing a character performance for short films and features.

Q: How do you go about getting the vital spark into your animation?

Ward Kimball: First of all, it starts with the story. Number two, if you have some entertaining business as you're telling the story, you know that's going to make your work look good. Then as you get into the animation itself, you do things that will improve the situation or sequence... you can add your own little touches that will enhance it... I animated to try and please the director by making his sequence work. But most of all, I animated to please myself. You've got to do that. Why do it if you're not pleased with it? If I'm not pleased, myself, that means there's something wrong with the design of the sequence. If I wasn't enthused right away and didn't want to start it, I'd say, 'There's something wrong here, maybe we'd better sit down and talk about it a little more... there are certain things that aren't working.'

You never know everything in advance when you start out on a character.... By animating a scene, even the first one, you make changes... because once you make a thing move or put it in action, it kind of dictates [design and acting] changes. You get ideas. It's sort of a growing process, and the more scenes you do, the more you know about the character. Unfortunately, when you've finished the picture, you wish you could go back and fix the first stuff because you've built the character. You've discovered little things that might be whimsical....

Anybody can animate to a certain degree, but the hardest thing in the world is to put your idea through. Even if it's crazy, it has to work within its own rules and be correct in order for you to get the most out of it.

– Ward Kimball interview with Nancy Beiman (1979)

Character development in an animated series

In Chapter 2, we saw how Art Babbitt developed an acting style for characters in short theatrical cartoons that ran for seven or eight minutes and commercials that ran for one minute (see page 44). Babbitt based his performances on written analyses of the character's motivations and personality. This was an uncommon method at the time but has now become standard procedure for feature film character development.

Short film series 'starring' the same character ran for years and gave the animators ample time to develop animated characters' personalities through trial and error. Bugs Bunny and Daffy Duck were character 'types' in their first films. They developed depth as their appearance and character changed over time. They also, uniquely among animated stars, 'performed' differently in films produced simultaneously in different directorial units at the Warner studio.

Chuck Jones interpreted Daffy Duck as an insecure coward who was insanely jealous of Bugs Bunny. Jones' Bugs was a cool, restrained character. Friz Freleng's Bugs Bunny could find himself at a disadvantage when pitted against a violent villain – though he always won in the end. Freleng's Daffy was foolish, but not jealous of Bugs. Bob Clampett's Daffy was completely crazy and uninhibited. His Bugs Bunny was short-tempered, aggressive, and occasionally defeated by an enterprising turtle or gremlin. The audience accepted these different interpretations as multiple facets of the same character. (It is true that these films were not meant to be seen one after the other, but it was possible for contemporary audiences to see different directorial interpretations of Bugs and Daffy in theatrical cartoons released in the same year. Cartoons were also re-released years after they were made and screened in compilations as early as the 1940s, according to my parents Melvyn and Frances Beiman, who attended Saturday matinees that included six or more Warner cartoons before the feature.)

Television series such as *The Simpsons* (1989–present) also offer an opportunity to have characters grow and develop depth over time. During the programme's long run the main characters' personalities changed (although Homer was always reassuringly consistent in his stupidity) and secondary Springfield citizens' characters were developed. This created new conflicts and relationships that took the show in different directions. It's almost a given that a long-running animated series in any medium must grow and change the characters to avoid repetition, though there have been successful series that did not. Chuck Jones' *Road Runner and Coyote* (1949–1994) cartoons immediately come to mind; the relationship and personalities of the two leads remained absolutely constant in every cartoon.

TIP

Webisodes and character development

Continuing characters on the Web can also develop their personalities over time, sometimes in very short episodes. *Simon's Cat* by Simon Tofield is an excellent Web cartoon series that caricatures familiar cat behaviour.

Character development in a commercial series

Animated commercials can also develop into a series with recognisable characters, though the acting may be a bit standard since the character usually displays a positive attitude about the product at all times. (There have been amusing 'negative ads' where this is not the case – these are the most fun to animate!)

Sometimes the commercial character develops a personality when the ad compresses a 'short film' story into a much shorter running time. Cartoon ads can feature a comic character getting into predicaments and out of them in thirty seconds, using stories that could appear in a longer cartoon but are simple enough to be understood in the ultra-short format. In the 60-second commercial *Snowdrift John and Marsha* (analysed in Chapter 2), Babbitt, writer Stan Freberg, and director John Hubley implied what happened *before* and *after* the onscreen action. This gave the acting depth despite the film's brief length and short production time.

Video game acting: New media, old methods

An animated performance for a feature, short film, or commercial runs for a set time and has a beginning, middle and end. Video game characters work within a time frame that is set by the player rather than the animator. The player is an unscripted additional character in the scenario; video games are interactive by nature.

Video games once featured mostly simple repeat cycle animation. Games have more recently been incorporating more and more narrative into their structure. This is a challenging prospect since character powers and the pace of the game are directly related to the skills of the player, and scenes cannot be planned to run identically each time as in a linear story.

Cut scenes or in-game cinematics reward the player for completing tasks, provide clues for the next level of the game and build character and story development. Video-game companies also produce trailers similar to the ones created for feature-film productions. These are distributed online in order to introduce viewers (including non-gamers) to the characters before the game is released. Animator/director Jamaal Bradley discussed the similarities between feature and video game animation in an interview with me in 2009:

Q: Do games animators need the same acting skills as a feature or television animator?

Jamaal Bradley: In the animation industry in general, things are becoming more competitive. Having had the privilege of working as a feature animator as well as a game animator, I can see how both have benefited my skill set. I would recommend ANY animator to learn acting skills to enhance their understanding of human movement. There will be 'go to' people for certain acting and action shots because not everyone has the same level of skill in every venue of animation, but there will be times that you have to step up and do various animation styles. With that being said, the lines are becoming more and more blurred as technology advances. Some game studios have the same number of people working on a project as the award-winning feature houses. I feel that if you are going to pursue an animation career you will need to be prepared to have your work be at a high level no matter if you are in feature, television, direct to DVD, commercial or games. Good animation is good animation no matter the industry.

Q: What is your opinion of games stories? Do you see them becoming sufficiently complex to develop strong characters, similar to those in a film? Has this already happened?

Jamaal Bradley: Video games have come a long way and the stories have become deeper. The hardest thing for game storytelling is incorporating a good story into an interactive world without taking the player out or disrupting the experience. The characters are complex, but how do you really show the depth of this simulated human and push that into the player's mind; actually making the player believe they are that person? Some games have done this with success and some have failed. Telling stories outside of the game and keeping it within the realm of the product opens an entire new experience for the players and even lets people who do not play games enjoy the world and characters.

Storytelling is definitely getting better in games and most studios are trying to push the envelope in this area. Many feature houses are trying to incorporate making games and films simultaneously. There are a lot reasons for this, but I see bigger signs of most production houses working together and building bigger projects that will be story heavy. Many game designers approach their development as an interactive cinema experience and have created some fantastic results. In due time games and film will have the same quality of characters and animation.

We never thought of the characters as drawings. We thought of them as living creatures.

– Chuck Jones, lecture at the California Institute of the Arts (1976)

Inspiration and reference

Books

1. Gesture drawing and thumbnails

Drawn to Life: 20 Golden Years of Disney Master Classes: The Walt Stanchfield Lectures, Volumes 1 and 2, by Walt Stanchfield, edited by Don Hahn (Focal Press, 2009) are recommended without reservation to all animators and animation students, for meticulous instruction in the art of capturing quick movement through thumbnails.

Force: Dynamic Life Drawing for Animators by Mike Mattesi (Focal Press, 2006) is a good guide to gestural drawing of human anatomy.

2. Animation technique and performance

Preston Blair's *Cartoon Animation* (Walter Foster Books, 1994) is the first animation textbook, and, though dated, still contains much useful material.

Frank Thomas and Ollie Johnston's *Disney Animation: The Illusion of Life* (Abrams, 1981) is an encyclopedic guide to Disney animation, story, and performance techniques from the Golden Age.

Chuck Reducks: Drawing from the Fun Side of Life* by Chuck Jones (Time Warner International, 1996) contains a unique guide to the Warner Brothers animators' performance style. (*Out of print but available on used book sites.)

The Animator's Workbook: Step-By-Step Techniques of Drawn Animation by Tony White (Watson-Guptill, 1988) is an excellent guide to basic animation techniques. Its well-planned exercises feature a generic human character.

Tony White's *Animation from Pencils to Pixels: Classical Techniques for the Digital Animator* (Focal Press, 2006) transposes hand-drawn methodologies to digital media.

Character Animation Crash Course! by Eric Goldberg (Silman-James Press, 2008) is an excellent guide to cartoon distortion, caricature, and action analysis.

Richard Williams' *The Animator's Survival Kit* (Faber and Faber, 2002) is a 'classical' analysis of animated action, with extensive explanations of technical processes.

Shamus Culhane includes valuable acting exercises in *Animation: From Script To Screen* (St. Martin's Griffin, 1990)

The acting methods and techniques of a stop-motion animator are described in Barry Purves' *Stop Motion: Passion, Process, and Performance* (Focal Press, 2007)

Basics Animation: Drawing for Animation by Paul Wells, Joanna Quinn and Les Mills (AVA Publishing, 2008) contains excellent drawings and thumbnails from a variety of animation media, with extensive illustrations from Quinn's own films.

3. Animals and vegetables

Ken Hultgren's *The Art of Animal Drawing: Construction, Action Analysis, Caricature* (Dover Publications, 1993) is a good source for Disney-influenced caricatured animal motion.

The changing stance of Tyrannosaurus and the ten-year-long reconstruction of the American Museum of Natural History's Halls of Vertebrate Evolution are described in *Next of Kin: Great Fossils at the American Museum of Natural History** by Lowell Dingus (Rizzoli, 1996.) (*Out of print but available on used book sites.)

Vegetable and animal are mixed and matched photographically in *Play with Your Food* (Stewart, Tabori and Chang, 1997) *Food Play* (Chronicle Books, 2006), and other books by Joost Elffers and Saxton Freymann.

4. Story context for performance

Making Shapely Fiction by Jerome Stern (W.W. Norton and Company, 1991) entertainingly explains how story affects character motivation.

My earlier book *Prepare to Board! Creating Story and Characters for Animated Features and Shorts* (Focal Press, 2007) describes how story influences character design and movement, and is a useful companion to the present volume.

Animation

Strange and fantastic animated creatures populate Elliot Cowan's *The Stressful Adventures of Boxhead and Roundhead* at: <http://www.elliotelliotelliot.com/br.html>

Doug Compton's *Cartoonal Knowledge* literally transforms the standard 'flour sack' exercise. His work can be seen here: <http://www.karmatoons.com/>

Dean Yeagle's animation-based gestural caricatures of animals and lovely girls can be viewed at: <http://cagedbeagle.com/>

Cat behaviour and movement is wittily caricatured in Simon Tofield's short animated films featuring *Simon's Cat* and the occasional dog: <http://www.simonscat.com/>

Bill Plympton's Oscar-nominated *Guard Dog* and two other films featuring a hilariously incompetent bouncing bulldog can be viewed on his *Dog Days* DVD, available at: <http://www.plymptoons.com>

Carlo Vogele's blog explains the methods used to produce stop-motion animation of clothing in *For Sock's Sake*: <http://carlovogele.blogspot.com/>

Animator PES uses a variety of inanimate objects to create new characters and textures in short animated films: <http://www.eatpes.com>

Jamaal Bradley's cut scene for *Team Fortress 2: Meet the Demoman* can be viewed here: <http://store.steampowered.com/app/997/>

Joanna Quinn's Oscar-nominated *Famous Fred* (1996) brilliantly combines feline and human caricature action.

Photographic reference

The *Sauropod Vertebra Picture of the Week* is an amusingly written, accessible guide to the latest developments in Sauropod dinosaur research: <http://svpow.wordpress.com/>

Many wonderful nature photographs have been put in the public domain on the Free Public Domain Photo Database: <http://www.pdphoto.org/index.php>

There are books and websites about individual animators and performers and extra features on many animation DVDs – too many to include here. Some examples are cited in specific chapters of *Animated Performance*. You will find many more. Lists are necessarily finite, but animation's potential is infinite.

Goodbye and good luck.

Index

Page numbers in *italics* refer to illustrations.

WITHDRAWN

Acknowledgements

The author owes much to the many people who contributed to this book. I thank Georgia Kennedy and her team at AVA Publishing for superb editing and production.

Director Yvette Kaplan provided outstanding professional reviews and critiques of my writing that resulted in a greatly improved text. This book truly would not have been the same without her input.

Supervising Animator Ellen Woodbury answered my questions in depth and sent a wealth of thumbnails and notes explaining her acting process on two Disney characters.

My former student Jamaal Bradley's interview and artwork provide unique perspectives on modern feature and game animation.

I thank the great animation artists, now gone, whom I interviewed or spoke with long before this book began: Arthur 'Art' Babbitt, Wolfgang 'Woolie' Reitherman, Ward Kimball, Isidore 'Friz' Freleng, and Charles M. 'Chuck' Jones.

I would also like to thank Margaret Adamic, Don Hahn, and Maggie Gisel at Walt Disney Enterprises; Sheridan students Adriana Pucciano, Domee Shi, Chang Dai, Hyein Park and Jean Park for their storyboards and life drawings; Sheridan life drawing professor Mark Thurman for the 'anatomical' flour sack; RIT graduate Ignacio Barrios for his CGI ape; RIT graduate Brittney Lee for her mermaid drawings; Carlo Vogele for the quote and stills from his Cal Arts film *For Sock's Sake*; Elliot Cowan for *Boxhead and Roundhead* and the rag doll, chair, and fish illustrations; Nina Haley for the portrait of Gizmo, Buddy, and Roswell; Barbara Dale for the scarecrow; Dean Yeagle for the life drawing with drapery; Doug Compton for animation drawings from *Cartoonal*

Knowledge; Simon Ward-Horner for the Were-Girl illustrations; Joanna Quinn and Beryl Productions for the *Body Beautiful* still; Hans Perk of A-Film for stills of *Snowdrift: John and Marsha*; Jerry Beck for fact-checking my anecdote about Mae Questel; the American Museum of Natural History for photos of their 1915 Tyrannosaurus mount; the artists who graciously shared their nature photographs through Creative Commons licences; and Associate Dean Angela Stukator and Dean Michael Collins of Sheridan College's Bachelor of Animation Arts program for their support and encouragement.

Index compiled by:
Indexing Specialists (UK) Ltd,
Indexing House,
306A Portland Road,
Hove,
East Sussex
BN3 6LP
Tel: 01273 416777
email: indexers@indexing.co.uk

187969